A marvelously stimulating book. Joh
derbrush" that has to be cleared away
market, both pro and con. Bolt doe
so with much theological wisdom (drawing helpfully on the 19ᵗʰ-century
neo-Calvinist tradition) and appropriate caution on matters where caution is often seriously lacking. We need this book—I hope it gets widely
discussed!

Richard J. Mouw
Professor of Faith and Public Life
Fuller Theological Seminary

Thoughtful and grounded in the Word, this primer should awaken those
hypnotized by the folly of the world to see a brighter tomorrow. Rather
than seeing our work and wealth as fodder for war, Dr. Bolt affirms that
both redound to the glory of God, Whose image we all bear. Drawing
from the wisdom of Kuyper and Bavinck, *Economic Shalom* is faithful to
God's Word and helpful to all those who call upon His name.

R. C. Sproul, Jr.
Associate Professor of Systematics and Philosophy
Reformation Bible College
Sanford, Florida

Economic Shalom is a thoughtful, carefully argued treatise in defense of
ordered liberty. Bolt provides a rare combination of deep theological reflection and sound economic thinking in his analysis of the world of
work, social structures, and political economy. I recommend this title to
anyone who wants an articulate integration of the Christian faith, cou-
pled with an excellent understanding of economic reality.

P. J. Hill
Professor Emeritus of Economics, Wheaton College
Senior Fellow, Property and Environment Research Center

In the midst of a cacophony of discordant voices touting the latest utopian visions of economic flourishing for all, *Economic Shalom* is a welcome and delightfully exhilarating breath of fresh air, filled with accessible biblical wisdom and hopeful realism. Peering through the illuminating lens of a robust Reformation tradition, the author graciously confronts the misguided pied pipers of class envy, toxic guilt, material scarcity, and coercive wealth redistribution. Emphasizing human dignity, individual liberty, wise stewardship, virtuous citizenry, free markets, and the power of gospel transformation, John Bolt does a masterful job of calling the church to vocational faithfulness, generous Christian compassion, and the fostering of economic opportunity for all. This book is essential reading for every thoughtful follower of Jesus who is serious about vocational faithfulness, the common good, and human flourishing. I highly recommend it!

Tom Nelson
Senior Pastor, Christ Community Church, Leawood, Kansas
Author of *Work Matters*

It is fitting for a systematic theologian to tackle the issue of economic systems. As a result this book presents the reader with a rich overview of what the Holy Scriptures, and especially Jesus, have to say about daily social problems and material needs. Bolt turns our attention back to the biblical message and seeks to restore the rich diaconal role of the church, which has in so many ways been usurped by the socialist state. And in the process Bolt challenges denominational leaders to think about the tendency to change the church into a social justice club. Bolt's overriding aim is to preserve a free society, a free church, and a free school in the Kuyperian tradition.

Rimmer de Vries
former chief economist and managing director, JP Morgan

If you are interested in a succinct, practical explanation of economics from a Christian perspective, this is the book. John Bolt masterfully explains and integrates profound biblical insights with a wide range of important economic literature from Augustine to Thomas Sowell and from Ron Sider to Paul Ehrlich. Posing frequently asked questions, he deftly weaves straightforward, compelling answers. You will gain a clearer understanding of the heritage of American capitalism and its necessity today.

Luder Whitlock
President, Excelsis Center
Executive Director, CNL Charitable Foundation

There is no shortage of books offering Christian perspectives on economics, but readers will make a big mistake if they conclude that John Bolt's new volume is dispensable. Prof. Bolt has written a truly outstanding work that deserves to be ranked among the very best on this intimidating but important topic. He lays exactly the right kind of theological foundation, a foundation that portrays human beings as responsible and creative image-bearers of God, that stresses biblical principles without forsaking the importance of natural revelation, and that does not confuse the economic life of this world with the coming of Christ's kingdom. Bolt combines this theological foundation with a wealth of economic wisdom that powerfully demonstrates the moral soundness and practical benefits of the market economy, alongside an evident concern for the poor and what they really need in order to escape poverty. I recommend this book with enthusiasm and hope that many will take its prescriptions to heart.

David VanDrunen
Robert B. Strimple Professor of Systematic Theology and Christian Ethics
Westminster Seminary, California

Primers in This Series

ECONOMIC
SHALOM

ECONOMIC SHALOM

A Reformed Primer on Faith, Work, and Human Flourishing

JOHN BOLT

With a Foreword by
David H. Kim

GRAND RAPIDS · MICHIGAN

ISBN: 978-1-938948-18-3

Christian's Library Press
An imprint of the Acton Institute for the Study of Religion & Liberty
98 E. Fulton Street
Grand Rapids, Michigan 49503
www.clpress.com

Cover and interior design by Sharon VanLoozenoord
Editing by Stephen J. Grabill, Timothy J. Beals, and Paul J. Brinkerhoff

22 21 20 19 18 17 16 15 14 13   1 2 3 4 5 6 7 8 9 10

Printed in the United States of America
First edition

Contents

Foreword

As a pastor in New York City, I work with Christians who yearn to make sense of their world. They actively engage their work because in it they find a strong sense of meaning. Unfortunately, these Christians often struggle with how to connect their faith with the world they actually inhabit for the vast majority of their waking hours. Many have grown up in churches that have essentially taught them that the only things that really matter in the end are saved souls. The net result of this kind of thinking is a disenfranchising dissociation between two important parts of their lives—their faith and their work. Over time, this tension inevitably fades as the increasing irrelevance of the Christian message often leads them to abandon not their faith, but the church.

There exists a deep hunger amongst Christians for an authentic faith that integrates the whole of life, connecting sincere piety with the complex public reality that people face each day. Six years ago I was hired by Redeemer Presbyterian Church to launch what became a nine-month leadership program for young professionals, focusing upon theological, spiritual, and community formation and integration. Participants would have to commit significant time and financial resources to be a part of the program. With considerable amounts of reading each week, as well as three challenging projects, we initially wondered whether over-scheduled, commitment-adverse New Yorkers would actually sign up for a program like this. In the last six years we were surprised to discover the answer to that question has been a resounding yes.

What has been profoundly reinforced in my mind over the years is that *theology matters.* When people discover a rich theology that connects what they have previously perceived as unrelated and irreconcilable parts of their lives, they experience a renewed passion for their faith and their work. Christians become excited about the gospel in a whole new way because they see how this hope applies not only to their own hearts and relationships but also to the world around them. They start to see how their work connects to the flourishing of the city and how the choices they make each day can have important economic implications. They begin to realize that the gospel does indeed speak powerfully into the economics of our modern, complex, pluralistic, multi-cultural world.

There is an overwhelming need for a deep and nuanced theology that articulates the reasons for the hope we have in Christ in every sphere of life. I have been greatly encouraged over the years to see churches from diverse denominational backgrounds desiring to deepen their theological resources. They too realize that faith and work integration requires a lot more than simply new programs, conferences, and studies. They want to ground Christians in a biblically rich framework that integrates the whole of their lives. In the past, typically para-church organizations have responded to this need, but I am seeing a whole new wave of churches that are taking up this charge to equip their people theologically and vocationally. This is an exciting movement because this kind of integration becomes much more effective when it's reinforced and lived in a dynamic community.

To this end, the book you hold in your hands is a very helpful primer, but don't mistake primer to mean elementary. As you will quickly discover, it is theologically rich and deep. While it doesn't promise to give you quick and easy answers, it will open your eyes to a way of connecting the Bible to our world today. This is not an easy task, and we need a skilled guide like John Bolt, whose mind has been deeply soaked in Scripture, and the best articulations of the Reformed faith from theologians like John Calvin, Abraham Kuyper, and Herman Bavinck. I hope this is the first of a score of books that will help bridge the gulf that exists for many between the Bible and our world today. I am deeply grateful for gifted theologians like Bolt who bring to life God's sovereignty over the whole of this world.

David H. Kim
Executive Director, The Center for Faith & Work
Redeemer Presbyterian Church, NYC
September 2013

Preface

When Stephen Grabill invited me to write the Reformed volume in this series of primers on work and economics, it took only a few moments of reflection to accept. In terms of my own writing, this volume parallels an earlier book, *The Christian Story and the Christian School* (1993), which was also a commissioned book that afforded me an opportunity to gather into one coherent narrative numerous essays, speeches to teachers' conventions, Christian school societies, and professional development days for Christian school teachers and administrators. Similarly, over the last two decades, I have been privileged to participate in numerous events at the Acton Institute and Acton University as listener/learner and as speaker/learner. I have written about and lectured on the role of Christian faith in the public square, including economics, and have focused my scholarly work on the neo-Calvinist thought of Abraham Kuyper, and especially Herman Bavinck. These are my credentials as well as my passions.

I write as one who has been nurtured and nourished within the Reformed catholic Christian faith more broadly and in Dutch neo-Calvinism more particularly. I include the adjective "catholic" here deliberately in company with my own teacher Herman Bavinck, who believed that being Reformed meant that one was a small *c* catholic Christian. In one of his magisterial addresses, "The Catholicity of Christianity and the Church" (1888), Bavinck made his case for considering the Reformed branch of Christianity as an expression of a comprehensive, all-inclusive faith that permeates every dimension of our existence as God's image bearers living in the creation he fashioned for his glory and human flourishing. The

Christian and Reformed faith is a comprehensive and public faith in the Triune God who created all things, redeems us in Christ, and in the power of the Holy Spirit is bringing all things to their final eschatological glory. I share that commitment and vision and this primer attempts to honor it.

It is a distinct privilege and responsibility for me to direct my attention especially to work and economics as a vital part of our Christian civic responsibility. I am a seminary teacher and now primarily a listener to sermons rather than an active preacher. I have long had a concern that ministers in the denomination I serve be better informed about basic economics. We devote a great deal of our denominational time and financial resources to issues of social justice and poverty/hunger in particular. God be praised for the compassionate hearts and willing hands that reach out to hungry and hurting people. But compassion ought to be informed; good intentions often have unintended consequences that make things worse by, among other things, creating dependency and destroying initiative. This is particularly true when global judgments are made and major structural changes are advocated in the name of the church. And that is why I have written this little book. My goal is to raise questions, to encourage second thoughts, and to invite discussion. I hope to educate, encourage, inspire, and motivate all Reformed Christians to a more informed discipleship in their vocations and civic responsibilities.

I am not an economist but a theologian, and this volume is not a substitute for picking up a basic economics text like Thomas Sowell's *Basic Economics* or a superb Christian perspective on economics such as Victor Claar and Robin Klay's *Economics in Christian Perspective*. With all due respect to Christian economists, I do not necessarily consider this a deficiency or a sin against academic sphere sovereignty. After all, the purpose of this series of books is not to contribute to social science scholarship but to inform lay Christian audiences of the connection between our Christian faith and the world of work and economics. If someone who is not an economist cannot explain that connection, then non-economists are not likely to be able to understand it. I believe that the key elements of economics can be understood and explained by anyone who has the desire to do so.

Of course, I do not claim that *understanding* the basics, and *knowing* the required conditions for economic flourishing will necessarily and easily lead to societies that actually accomplish it. And here the help of theology is essential; economists need theologians as much as theologians who write about faith and work need economists. What does the Christian faith teach us about human nature? How does the reality of sin affect the degree to which we can achieve economic shalom in this dispensation? If we reject an eschatological reserve and demand more than can be achieved in this life, how do we then—with every good intention in place!—avoid the horrific track record of failed utopias that spill oceans of blood and create mountains of misery? Mistakes in advocacy, especially when done in the name of Christ, have terribly serious consequences, not the least because they discredit the gospel itself. I write, therefore, as a theologian with a strong interest in matters of public polity and economy who has a modest track record of teaching and publication in the area.

A brief word or two is in order about my own journey and particular intellectual debts in the area of economics. I came to Calvin College and Seminary in the late 1960s as a Canadian student with certain typically Canadian biases against the American experiment in ordered liberty. At the same time, the Dutch-Canadian immigrant community in which I grew up was politically unsophisticated but generally conservative and definitely not socialist. Post–World War II experiences with an increasingly bureaucratically ordered life had definitely shaped that bias. However, during my college and seminary years, the Vietnam War and especially the American civil rights movement so dominated the public world of my student life that I was gently drawn to aspects of the countercultural critique of America as the lead society of the capitalist West. In particular, the problem of world hunger and the imperative of a simple lifestyle that rejected consumerism captured my imagination and moral conscience. The so-called "American way" troubled me; I was tentatively drawn to Christian socialism as an alternative.

All that changed for me in the 1980s. Remarkably, I was initially disappointed in Ronald Reagan's victory over Jimmy Carter in the US presidential election of 1980. At the same time, the killing fields of Southeast Asia after the American pullout were troubling, and my reading turned to those who presented the moral case against twentieth-century totalitarianism—people such as Alexandyr Solzhenitsyn (*One Day in the Life of Ivan Denisovich* and *The Gulag Archipelago*), Armando Valladares (*Against All Hope: The Prison Memoirs*), and Nien Cheng (*Life and Death in Shanghai*). At the same time, other writers, such as Malcolm Muggeridge (*Winter in Moscow*) and Paul Hollander (*Political Pilgrims: Travels of Western Intellectuals to the Soviet Union, China, and Cuba, 1928–1978*) directed me to the troubling and tragic romance that left-leaning Western intellectuals had with totalitarianism, all in the name of a more just and fair world. As I saw my own church in Canada increasingly insert itself into national and global political and economic issues, I began to wonder if much of that arose from the same romance with utopian visions of the kingdom of God on earth. Though it appealed to the legacy of Abraham Kuyper, it did not strike me as very compatible with the Kuyperian understanding of the church's task. I did not yet, however, have a clear, well worked out alternative.

Dissatisfaction with Christian socialism, furthermore, did not satisfy my moral concerns about a more just social and economic order. Then I read Michael Novak's *The Spirit of Democratic Capitalism*. Novak set forth what he called "a theology of economics" in which he made a persuasive case for a threefold cord of free-market economies operating in democratic societies with healthy moral-cultural institutions. Here was a complete vision, rooted in liberty, with a high view of human beings as responsible image bearers of God, and that had, furthermore, proved itself as an engine for prosperity. This was the vision of a moral political economy I had been looking for; moreover, it was realistic and anti-utopian. It was, in Novak's words, "a political economy for sinners." In addition to Novak, Peter Berger and Richard John Neuhaus's work on mediating structures in public policy (*To Empower People*) became for me a helpful new language for translating the insights of the neo-Kuyperian tradition into the North American context. After returning to live in Grand Rapids in 1989, this is what drew me to the Acton Institute after it was founded in 1990, and I have been honored to participate in many of its events, including representing Calvin Theological Seminary in sharing the sponsorship of a successful conference in October 1998, "The Legacy of Abraham Kuyper and Leo XIII: Commemorating over a Century of Christian Social Teaching." And finally, for ongoing and lasting influence, I would single out the thinker I judge to be the most important "public intellectual" in America today, the economist Thomas Sowell. Not only does Sowell make economics understandable, he explains real-world economic results in terms of a realistic anthropology with moral and cultural values that always ring true.

My colleagues, students, and friends will undoubtedly respond in bemusement that I have written a book that includes the word "shalom" in the title. I have on more than one occasion commented that the word is overused today. In my defense, the title preceded the request to write. However, I never raised an objection to the title and see this volume as something of a gentle corrective to much of the writing that has filled the shalomological genre in recent years. If I may put it directly, my own intention was to write a book that describes and outlines *real-world shalom*, shalom as achievable and already achieved in part rather than an ideal shalom that is only future eschatological (or worse, utopian) hope. This opens up opportunity for conversation and dialogue because people of goodwill do disagree about what is achievable. This volume, therefore, is not intended as the last word on the subject, and I know that even close friends and colleagues will find points with which to disagree. I welcome that, in fact, because I have found over and over again that we never grow in our understanding by only "preaching to the choir." My purpose in writing is similar; I am writing on behalf of Her Majesty's loyal opposition here since the overwhelming weight of ecclesiastical writing and practice looks at the world of economics, commerce, and markets in quite a different way.

I am confident that good conversation about these issues is possible because an invaluable part of the experience of writing this book came from my request to student members of the Calvin Theological Seminary Social Justice Club if they would be willing to read a penultimate draft and discuss it with me. Herewith my thanks to Bryant De Kruyter, Adrian De Lange, Brandon Haan, Shannon Jamal-Hollemans, Jin Li, Micah Schuurman, and David Zigterman for your willingness to serve as *my* loyal opposition. Your openness, honesty, and probing questions have made this a better book. It is also better than it would have been without the friendship and contribution of Henry Vander Goot, who brought to our ongoing conversations over the years about the issues in this book the rare and helpful combination of intellectual/academic gift and successful entrepreneurial experience. Henry's careful reading of my first draft of each chapter was encouraging and constructive. Many of the nuances that are in the final edition need to be credited to his thoughtful interaction with my writing. After I had completed and submitted what I thought of as my final draft, two friends and colleagues, Stephen Grabill of the Acton

Institute and Greg Forster of the Kern Family Foundation, read the entire manuscript and provided really valuable advice for nuance and correction. Though it meant a few more days of work for me, the advice was spot on target and makes the final manuscript much better. I am grateful to God for the sympathetic community and constructive honest advice by way of the many helpful questions and suggestions I received from all of those mentioned above.

I have dedicated this book to a dear friend, Harry Antonides, whose Christian commitment, dedication to the work of Christian social and political analysis, and courage to speak up for and defend the Reformed faith when it was not easy to do so, remain an inspiration to me. I also want to highlight and acknowledge the many men and women who, like Harry, have been involved with the *Christian Labour Association of Canada* over the sixty years that *CLAC* has been an exemplary instrument of social justice in Canada and faithful witness to the importance of faith in the workplace. This Dutch-Canadian-American Reformed theologian salutes you.

Note to reader: Each chapter is followed by "Discussion Questions" and suggestions "For Further Reading." In lieu of footnotes or endnotes, parenthetical references (author, title, and page number) are given in the text. Though works may be referenced in subsequent chapters, the full bibliographic information will not be repeated but given only in shortened form. For ease of reference, all titles are provided in a final bibliography.

Introduction

"Follow the Money"—What Is Economics All About?

[Everything looks different] when considered from the standpoint of allocating scarce resources which have alternate uses.
Thomas Sowell

The economist comes before his fellow citizens with the bad news of scarcity—as the production of goods increases, so does demand and desire—hence the Kingdom of God will never come to earth through economic means.
Wilhelm Röpke

[Economics is] [n]ot "gay science," I should say, like some we have heard of; no, a dreary, desolate and, indeed, quite abject and distressing one; what we might call, by way of eminence, *the dismal science*.
Thomas Carlyle

Cub reporters eager to make their mark in journalism are often told by veterans on the job to "follow the money." The point of the advice is to encourage investigative journalists not to be satisfied with the obvious and to refuse to accept surface explanations and motivations. While the advice may be sound, it also has the effect of fueling profound cynicism about all human behavior. It assumes that all noteworthy human motivations are reducible to some kind of financial calculation. After all, if everything finally comes down to inward-looking self-interest, to getting more for oneself, to accumulating wealth or power, very little is left for other motivations that can be described as true, noble, good, and lovely.

When we turn to investigate economics itself—where *inward-looking* or self-serving profit is thought to be the very point of the activity—suspicion and cynicism seem natural and are often intensified. For many, some Christians included, "following the money" are a matter of course here because they view economic life itself, especially modern global capitalism, with varying degrees of distrust. According to one such critic, "covetousness is the engine of the capitalist economy." Another critic claims that capitalism "depends on and fosters human selfishness." Sojourners founder Jim Wallis gathers together a number of nasty descriptors into one huge pile of judgment: capitalist "economic institutions act to make profit, accumulate wealth, and exploit the poor, workers, and consumers, while ravaging the environment instead of providing for the equitable distribution of goods and services" (quoted in Craig M. Gay, *With Liberty and Justice for Whom?* 23–24). From this description it would seem unthinkable that a follower of Christ could speak positively about the economic system we know as capitalism. Is there an alternative to "following the money"?

Since we have no choice but to "follow the money" when we shine our spotlight on economics—money is what most people mistakenly think it's all about—we need to start with a less inflamed attitude. If we are to come to a healthy understanding of work, business, entrepreneurship, and civic responsibility, we will have to set aside whatever negative feelings we may have about economic life and determine to hold a more neutral posture. So without prejudice or suspicion or preconceived bias, let's examine economic life. With what kinds of human action is economics concerned? I will develop a full answer in a series of propositions that move from general descriptions to more specific. My goal is to

arrive at a normative definition, one that leads to human flourishing, recognizing that living in a fallen world means we will never
arrive at full and definitive economic shalom in this life.

1. Economics deals with the one aspect or dimension of human behavior that involves exchanging things of value.

Economics is not everything; everything is not economics. We need
to state this up front to help us avoid the mistake of reducing all
human behavior to economic self-interest. We also need to avoid
thinking that all things of value are reducible to a price point. Even
the words *profit* or *profitable* are not restricted to matters of mammon. Activities and habits that en*rich* our souls—music lessons,
reading good literature, a liberal arts education, etc.—are profitable even when costly from a financial point of view. Economics
is not everything; everything is not economics; profit is not just
about the bottom line.

What is economics about? Economics is concerned with those
human actions involving exchange. Now it is of course true that
thanks to our sinful hearts, even the most intimate and personal
human interaction can be tainted by economic considerations. A
young man in love wants a diamond ring for his beloved; a local
shop, Jewels Verne, sells diamond rings. The young man works,
saves money, purchases the ring, receives parental blessing, gets
on his knees, and "pops the question." The purchase of the ring
is economics; "popping the question" surely not. But, what if the
young man comes from poor peasant stock and the young lady is
a well-to-do heiress? In that case, significant economic considerations *could* enter into the picture, beginning with concerns the
young woman's family might raise about the purity of the young
man's motives. In the class-ridden societies of older Europe, such

relationships between nobility and commoner were not unheard of, but more often they were only fodder for "upstairs/downstairs" gossip and tut-tutting. Economics may not be everything, but economics has the possibility of casting its shadow over even the most intimate human relationship. Conversely, business people may decide to act in ways that do not maximize profit and make decisions that are not *primarily* governed by economic self-interest. Different values and ideals, such as love of family, concern about employees, love of community or nation, may override purely economic interests.

To say that everything is not economics does not remove the suspicions altogether and calls for careful discernment and charity. In the case of trying to understand the relation between Christian faith and economics, it requires spiritual discernment and neighbor-love. Christians are supposed to be "wise as serpents and innocent as doves" according to our Lord's instruction (Matt. 10:16). This calls for prudent judgments of charity; we must be appropriately cautious, but Christians violate the love command when they start out with attitudes of suspicion and hostility toward rich people. In economic terms, "keep your eyes on the balance sheets and love your neighbor as yourself."

The example of a young lover purchasing an engagement ring reminds us that "exchanging things of value" is not yet a full definition of economics. It also reminds us that economic activity is not a matter of "gift exchange." Economic activity involves exchange *for the sake of outward-looking profit*, that is to say, profit or blessing that is considered to be so by all parties to the transaction. This is an important point. Acts of economic exchange are mutually beneficial. That is why they are different from gift exchanges. A gift is gratuitous and generous; it does not expect a return except a "thank you." When someone gives a "gift" in a calculated gesture to gain profit for self, it has become something quite different—a bribe. Therefore, to fill out our definition we need to enter in the profit motive, understood now in the broad sense as *outward-looking profit*.

2. Economics deals with the one aspect or dimension of human behavior that involves exchanging things of value *for the sake of profit*.

Speaking of "profit" pushes to the very limit our earlier caution about leaving prejudices and biases behind for a more neutral posture. The word "profit" in our definition almost requires being placed in scare quotes, such is the hostility that it evokes in many people of high moral intention. This moral indignation is more than matched by the derision accompanying the term *self-interest*. A calmer and more measured response, however, recognizes that while *selfishness* is indeed sinful, self-interest is essential to our own survival. In fact we humans cannot stay alive without self-regard. Eating healthy food, exercising regularly, and getting sufficient sleep are all self-interested choices made by morally sound people daily. So, the economic act of person X exchanging his valuable possession for person Y's money is no less moral and fitting than choosing to eat vegetables instead of bacon rinds or French fries. In a phrase, *profit* is not a four-letter word. Neither is self-interest necessarily morally dubious.

Nonetheless, we need to ask further what lends value for profit to an economic activity. Here we take our analysis one additional step and note that the answer is *scarcity*. As economist Thomas Sowell has pointed out, speaking of economics as the science that studies the way humans produce goods and distribute goods and services is not enough: "The Garden of Eden was a system for the production and distribution of goods and services, but it was not an economy, because everything was available in unlimited abundance. Without scarcity, there is no need to economize— and therefore no economics" (*Basic Economics*, 2). Sowell then follows with the following classic definition of economics from British economist Lionel Robbins:

> Economics is the study of the use of scarce resources which have alternative uses.

INTERLUDE 1

Profit is not the only goal.

A Christian utopian dreamer once foolishly expressed a longing for a world in which General Motors would be interested in building good cars instead of making profits. The matter of profit in business is rather simple: only profitable businesses survive and are able to do good by providing goods and services to others. Unprofitable enterprises are inefficient and wasteful; profits are essential to good stewardship. At the same time, however, a Christian business person does need to think about more than profit alone. Business too is to be conducted for the glory of God, for the benefit of God's kingdom. Financial profit or the famous "bottom line" must never become an idol. This means that some very profitable business ventures—legal but morally dubious—are off limits for those who honor Christ as Lord. In addition, there may be certain types of business that are both legal and moral but reflect values of stewardship that do not promote the kingdom of God. There are products and services the world really does not need because they provide no human benefits beyond a job and opportunity for consumption. There are times when entrepreneurs also need to say no. Pet rocks, anyone? Business people are stewards of all that God entrusts to their care and, as they face choices, it is the well-being of God's kingdom that must take precedence over profits alone. This is a challenge and responsibility not unique to those in business; every disciple of Christ, no matter what his or her vocation, faces such lordship choices. Self-centered and self-serving choices are as serious a problem in the academy, in the helping professions, and, yes, even in the church, as they are in business.

Economists Victor Claar and Robin Klay note that awareness of scarcity is also a matter of Christian wisdom: "One of the fundamental assumptions economists make about human activity is that we are limited in our choices by scarce time, resources and knowledge. Christians acknowledge that reality." Furthermore, "although Christians are called to have 'faith that can move mountains,' they are taught not to defy gravity or tempt God by jumping from rooftops. Likewise, they would court physical and spiritual danger if they ignored real limits to their material and financial resources" (*Economics in Christian Perspective*, 15).

When we speak of "scarce resources that have alternative uses," we link economics to an important biblical theme—stewardship. Stewardship is a favorite theme of environmentalists—and properly so—but all too often forgotten is that stewardship involves *use*. Stewardship does not mean, in the first place, leaving God's creation alone to be preserved in its pristine form. "The earth is the LORD's, and the fullness thereof" (Ps. 24:1), but he has also given it to those who fear him with the promise that "his soul shall abide in well-being, and his offspring shall inherit the land" (Ps. 25:13). This leads us to our third formulation:

3. Economics deals with the one aspect or dimension of human behavior that involves *stewardly* exchanging *scarce things of value* for the sake of profit.

There is one additional normative element that needs to be added and will serve as a segue to the next chapter. The assumption in the preceding discussion has been that the mutually beneficial exchanges we are speaking of are not coerced but those of free and responsible human moral agents. Theft is an economic activity of sorts involving "scarce things of value," but it does not involve *mutual* exchange for profit. Theft is a zero-sum exchange; economics is not. This point is often overlooked by critics of free enterprise. The world economy is often portrayed, especially in ecumenical ecclesiastical pronouncements such as the World Communion of Reformed Churches' Accra Confession, as pure exploitation of the weak by the powerful, as a plundering of the poor by the rich. While it is undeniable that such exploitation has taken and does take place, it is simply untrue that free enterprise in a free and democratic society is a zero-sum exchange. We will forego a more complete look at this question until a later chapter, but we note it here so that we can come to our fourth formulation.

4. Economics is that study of the one aspect or dimension of human behavior that involves stewardly exchanging, *by free moral agents*, scarce things of value for the sake of profit.

Finally, in the interest of precision, the word "study" in our definition may be too general; we should introduce the notion of "science." A businessman who studies the demographics and known needs of his community, the goods offered by his competitor, the likelihood of profits, the potential risks, and so forth, is *studying* but, technically speaking, he is not yet an economist. The parallel here is with the vocation of *theologian*. In a rudimentary sense, all thoughtful, reflective Christians are amateur theologians. The vocation of theologian requires disciplined study, mastery of the tradition and traditions of the church's theological masters, and a more or less full-time dedication to the theological task. The same is true for the vocation or profession of an economist. This volume is neither a work of pure theology nor of pure economics; it is a work of reflection on matters of faith, economics, work, and civic responsibility. I will be using the fruit of economists along with that of Christian theologians, ethicists, and social thinkers to set forth a vision of flourishing life in the economic realm. But, I am proceeding from the conviction that the more general and broader understanding of economics is helpful here because even economics as a discipline is not in the first place a highly specialized and even mathematically quantifiable science but a *practical* and *moral* science. As Aristotle noted in his *Nicomachean Ethics*, practical sciences apply reason to *praxis*, to human action. This makes them far less exact than, say the physical sciences—"due to the contingency of human action deriving from its freedom and singularity" (Ricardo F. Crespo, "Controversy: Is Economics a Moral Science?" 202)—and makes prudential wisdom the most important quality of the practical scientist. Furthermore, "since human action is essentially free," it is "essentially moral" (Ibid.). This leads us to our fifth and final, normative definition of economics.

5. Economics is that *practical and moral scientific* study of the one aspect or dimension of human behavior that involves stewardly exchanging, *by free moral agents*, scarce things of value for the sake of profit.

This is a bare-bones definition of economics that does not include many things that go into economic activity, such as allocation and limits of resources, production and wages, markets, prices, demand and supply, and the list goes on. Many of these topics—albeit in a broad, general manner—will be addressed in the later chapters of this book in the context of key themes arising from Christian confession and commitment. The first part and next four chapters of this book are dedicated to exploring four of those key themes.

Discussion Questions

1. Prior to reading this chapter, did you think of the modern global economy in generally positive or negative terms? Why? Did the way this chapter defined economics change your view?

2. What are the most pressing questions you have about the economy and Christian discipleship?

3. Why is it important to distinguish *inward-looking profit* from *outward-looking profit*?

4. Using the apostle Paul's wise counsel that "'All things are lawful for me,' but not all things are helpful" (1 Cor. 6:12), can you think of any economic activity that may be legal and moral but is inadvisable for Christians?

5. Are you aware of a movement among younger evangelical Christians known as the "new asceticism"? What is your opinion of it? Do you favor "simple living"?

6. What specific "self" sins are the temptations of your vocation/profession?

For Further Reading

Claar, Victor V., and Robin J. Klay, *Economics in Christian Perspective: Theory, Policy and Life Choices.* Downers Grove, IL: InterVarsity Press, 2007.

Crespo, Ricardo F. "Controversy: Is Economics a Moral Science?" *Journal of Markets and Morality* 1, no. 2 (October 1998): 201–11. http://www.marketsandmorality.com/index.php/mandm/article/view/3/2.

Gay, Craig M. *With Liberty and Justice for Whom? The Recent Evangelical Debate over Capitalism.* Grand Rapids: Eerdmans, 1991.

Sirico, Robert. *Defending the Free Market: The Moral Case for a Free Economy.* Washington, DC: Regnery, 2012.

Sowell, Thomas. *Basic Economics: A Common Sense Guide to the Economy.* 4th ed. New York: Basic Books, 2011. First published in 2000.

Four Key Themes of Economics in Christian Confession and Commitment

"Does the Bible Really Teach That?"

Is There a "Biblical Economics"?

Both [North and South] read the same Bible and pray to the same God. . . .
The prayers of both could not be answered. That of neither has been
answered fully. The Almighty has His own purposes.
Abraham Lincoln, "Inaugural Address," March 4, 1865

The ancient agrarian world of the Bible seems far removed from our modern world where multinational corporations create wealth for people on each continent; communications satellites make it possible for lovers in Grand Rapids, Michigan, and Shanghai, China, to have face-to-face conversations via Skype; and oncology radiologists are able to send chemotherapeutic "bullets" into the bloodstream to destroy targeted cancer cells. On the face of it, the Bible would seem to offer little concrete direction for, let's say, a chief financial officer of a major bank, a lawyer specializing in international trade, a chief of surgery at a major research hospital, or a television producer.

Of course the Bible does offer modern people spiritual and moral guidance. People are still sinners and need the grace of God's forgiveness in Jesus Christ. The Ten Commandments remain relevant for presidents of nations, televangelists, and Hollywood celebrities as well as Sunday school children. But this is not the place we raise questions about the Bible's relevance for the complexities of our modern world. We want to know whether or not the Bible has anything to say about stem-cell research, free trade or fair trade, climate change, and minimum wage laws. And here the historical distance seems overwhelming. The default position would seem to discount the Bible's relevance to such issues. But serious Christians who are committed to the Bible's authority as the ultimate rule for life cannot be satisfied with such a dismissal. If we are not prepared to accept the modern Enlightenment divide between our private and public lives, we need to acknowledge that we face great challenges in applying the Bible to our daily lives of work and enterprise beyond obvious moral imperatives such as honesty, integrity, fairness, and mutual respect. This is a particular challenge for Reformed Christians whose theological tradition emphasizes integrating biblical faith with every dimension of human life.

Nonetheless, a number of Christian thinkers have taken up the challenge and directly and specifically applied biblical themes to modern economic realities and problems. Before proposing my own constructive answer to this question, I will examine several of the main answers given by way of a series of questions in the form of "Does the Bible teach this?" To keep the discussion brief, I will focus on four Christian thinkers whose views may overlap in some areas but whose basic presuppositions and perspectives are quite different: American Social Gospel theologian Walter Rauschenbusch, contemporary evangelical Ronald Sider, theonomist David Chilton, and Dutch neo-Calvinist Herman Bavinck. Though Rauschenbusch and Sider are not Reformed but come from the Baptist/Anabaptist tradition, both have been historically influential even in the broader Reformed community. And while it is true that Chilton represents a distinct minority position in the

Reformed world, his approach to Scripture serves as an instructive contrast to both Sider and Bavinck. Within the confines of this chapter, the treatment of key persons and issues will be descriptive and brief.

Question 1: Did Jesus' preaching point to socialism? Walter Rauschenbusch and the "Social Gospel"

No one jumped into the challenge of bringing the Bible into serious engagement with the realities of the modern industrial world as passionately and as thoroughly as the Baptist pastor and theologian Walter Rauschenbusch (1861–1918), whose major writings include such titles as *Christianity and the Social Crisis* (1907), *Christianizing the Social Order* (1912), and his crowning work, *Theology for the Social Gospel* (1917). Raised in an orthodox Protestant home, Rauschenbusch's seminary education at Rochester Theological Seminary, New York, led him to embrace a higher-critical approach to the Bible and to doubt the substitutionary atonement of Christ. However, rather than leaving the faith and a life of service in the church, he stayed and became one of the most influential twentieth-century leaders in revising Christianity itself.

Rauschenbusch found his key to reinterpreting the gospel, along with the answer to the social crisis of the day, in Jesus' teaching about the kingdom of God. While we must take issue with Rauschenbusch's theology and his economics, we must not minimize the urgency of the social crisis he faced with imagination and courage. The Industrial Revolution of the nineteenth century helped create a divided world of growing wealth and intensifying misery at the same time. It brought thousands of people from rural areas into the urban centers of Europe as cottage industries gave way to "factory" production. The result was a growing number of urbanized working poor who lived in squalid conditions and struggled to meet basic necessities of life. This was the world that serves as the background for Charles Dickens's novels and led English poet William Blake to pen his famous lines about "dark Satanic Mills."

The same thing happened to large North American cities and with similar tragic results. After finishing his studies in Germany, Rauschenbusch served for eleven years as a pastor in Hell's Kitchen, New York City, where he saw the horrors firsthand. Rauschenbusch turned his double dissatisfaction with traditional Christianity and the social-economic order of his day into a new social gospel of the kingdom of God. He portrayed Jesus as a revolutionary who "instituted the ideal republic" of social cooperation and love. While "Plato dreamed of an ideal republic, Christ instituted it." To this, he added: "The splendid principle of the French Revolution: 'Liberty, equality, fraternity,' contains the social principles of the church" (*The Righteousness of the Kingdom*, 172–73). "The fundamental purpose of Jesus," Rauschenbusch claimed, "was the establishment of the kingdom of God, which involved a thorough regeneration and reconstruction of social life" (*Christianity and the Social Crisis*, 143). What does this look like? It is characterized by "socializing property," something which Rauschenbusch defines as "made to serve the public good either by the services its uses render to the public welfare, or by the income it brings to the public treasury" (*Christianizing the Social Order*, 420). In simple terms: Jesus intended socialism with his preaching about the kingdom of God. Rauschenbusch's solution to the challenge of overcoming the historical gap between the Bible and modern economic life is to interpret Jesus' teaching about the kingdom of God as a direct call for revolutionizing the economic order itself.

It is appropriate to ask why we should pay attention to a thinker whose views—higher-critical approach to Scripture; denial of Christ's substitutionary atonement—are so clearly contrary to those of orthodox, conservative, evangelical, Reformed Christians. The reason will become clear when we consider the next thinker because Ronald Sider also takes Jesus' teaching about the kingdom of God as entailing a radical reordering of economic life in somewhat the same direction. It is this move from the biblical teaching about the kingdom of God to concrete, this-worldly politics and economics, held in common by Rauschenbusch and Sider, that has profoundly influenced even many Reformed Christians.

Question 2: Do rich people cause poverty, and is God on the side of the poor? Ronald J. Sider and "Jubilee" Redistribution

During the 1970s, a number of books were written to awaken North American evangelical Christians and their consciences to world hunger and their complicity in creating it. Included among these volumes were W. Stanley Mooneyham's *What Do You Say to a Hungry World?* (1975), Arthur Simon's *Bread for the World* (1975), and Ronald J. Sider's *Rich Christians in an Age of Hunger* (1977). The last-mentioned, which may have been the single most important book in evangelical social ethics during the last two decades of the twentieth century, set forth a vision of economic life that was echoed by a number of ecclesiastical reports such as the Christian Reformed Church's *And He Had Compassion on Them* (1978) and the US Roman Catholic Bishops Conference pastoral letter, *Economic Justice for All* (1986). This vision can be set forth in a series of axioms that follow in logical order:

Assumption: "Their" poverty is largely caused by "our" wealth.

Biblical teaching: In his ministry, Jesus showed that he was on the side of the poor.

Conviction: We must follow Jesus and imitate his love for the poor.

Implication: Following Jesus, who preached Jubilee (Luke 4), Christians must practice and promote redistribution of wealth from the rich to the poor.

Sider does want to be cautious in directly applying biblical teaching to economics today: "Although biblical revelation tells us that God and his faithful people are always at work liberating the oppressed, Scripture gives us no comprehensive blueprint for a new economic order" (*Rich Christians in an Age of Hunger*, 220). To which he then immediately adds: "We do find, however, important principles about justice in society." The principles he points to are, on the personal level, following the suggestion of the Club of Rome's report *Limits to Growth*, a "graduated tithe" whereby we voluntarily accept for ourselves a "more simple personal lifestyle" so in the end "everyone can share the good earth's bounty" lest "growing divisions between rich and poor . . . lead not only to more starvation and death but also to increasing civil strife, terrorism, and war," not to mention rapid depletion of our natural resources or environmental degradation (*Rich Christians in an Age of Hunger*, 187–90, 269). Sider also suggests a lifestyle of simplicity that might include more communal living instead, with financial sharing replacing individualized units of nuclear families.

But, significant structural change is also required. As Sider puts it, "An age of affluence and poverty demands compassionate action and simplicity in personal lifestyles. But compassion and simple living apart from structural change may be little more than a gloriously irrelevant ego trip or proud pursuit of personal purity" (220). While Sider first applies biblical teaching to the church, he insists that "the biblical vision of the coming kingdom suggests the kind of social order God wills." And, because "the biblical authors did not hesitate to apply revealed norms to persons and societies outside the people of God"—Isaiah denouncing Assyria; Amos prophesying judgment against Israel's neighbors; Daniel rebuking Nebuchadnezzar—Christians have every right to insist that the nations of the world pay attention to God's law as it is revealed in Scripture. Concretely, this means "a drastic reorientation of US foreign policy" toward "unequivocally siding with the poor"; encouraging "nonviolent movements working for structural change in developing countries"; and churches sending missionaries who will preach "the explosive biblical message that God has a special concern for the poor and oppressed" (209).

Furthermore, because God is the absolute owner of everything, "the human right to the resources necessary to earn a just living overrides any notion of absolute private ownership." And, since the God of the Bible "wills institutionalized structures (rather than mere charity) which systematically and regularly reduce the gap between the rich and the poor," Sider applies Old Testament Jubilee legislation to our day by way of Jesus's own application to himself in his Nazareth sermon (Luke 4). This implies that the United States should "drastically reduce or eliminate trade barriers on imports for developing nations," even granting them trade preference along with access to international "stabilization funds" that would guarantee maximum returns on key commodities. Other recommendations include federal government food programs that encourage appropriate consumption, and a turn in foreign aid away from military arms to food (205–18).

Like Rauschenbusch, Sider moves directly from biblical teaching to specific contemporary economic application. Jesus' teaching about the kingdom of God means a new social order and points to state intervention in redistributing wealth with a view toward greater equality of outcome. Though both men come from the Anabaptist/Baptist family of churches, the direction they suggest has also influenced many Reformed Christians and churches who today often sound Anabaptist when they engage in economic analysis and propose policies *in the name of the Reformed tradition*. This indicates some confusion among many Reformed people about what our tradition actually teaches.

We will now consider someone from the Reformed tradition who has offered a sharp and pointed critique of Sider while retaining Sider's biblicism. David Chilton believes that the Bible mandates free-market or capitalist economies. He will be the first of two Reformed thinkers we will consider because, his major disagreement with Sider notwithstanding, he also appeals directly to Old Testament law in an immediate move from biblical text to contemporary economic application. After that, we will consider the Dutch neo-Calvinist theologian Herman Bavinck.

Question 3: Are the economic laws of Old Testament Israel directly transferable to modern North America? David Chilton and Christian Reconstruction

Picking up Chilton's book *Productive Christians in an Age of Guilt-Manipulators* (1981) from a book table forces one to do a double take. It looks very much like the original edition of Sider's *Rich Christians in an Age of Hunger*, with the same color scheme and a title box that appears identical until a closer look reveals the provocative and quite different title. At this point, one is likely to conclude that someone has put out a mock "spoof edition" of Sider's book. That conclusion would be a mistake; though there is a definite "cheekiness" to Chilton's book and the tone is often sharp and even mocking, his critique is substantive and serious. My purpose here, however, is not to highlight Chilton as Sider's critic but to briefly consider his own constructive proposal about biblical law.

Chilton is a "theonomist," a follower of the Christian Reconstruction movement founded by Rousas John Rushdoony. The signature conviction of theonomists is the abiding validity of Old Testament biblical law, including its penal sanctions, for our life in modern America. And the economic system required by Scripture? Chilton states forthrightly: "My position is that the Bible calls for a free market in which the state does not intervene." He insists that this is not identical with "a 'pure' laissez-faire economic system in an anarchic or antinomian sense: the laws of the Bible do prohibit certain activities from taking place. Consenting adults are not the highest authority. But in the normal transactions of the market, the government must not interfere. Prices and wages are to be set by consumers in the context of supply and demand. The state does not subsidize certain industries, nor does it prohibit men from making a profit." This has profound implications for how we respond to people who are poor: "Charity is personal, though not purely 'voluntary,' since biblical law commands it—but on the other hand, those laws are not enforced by the state: the Bible mandates no civil penalties for failing to obey the charity laws" (*Productive Christians*, 35).

What is striking about Chilton's critique of Sider is that he takes identical biblical teaching and comes to diametrically opposite conclusions. He too starts with the premise that God is the Creator and absolute Owner of all things, but he insists that "the point of the biblical emphasis on *God's* ownership is that all property must be held in strict accordance with His commands." Chilton grants that this places divinely instituted limits on what individual property owners can do with their property, but the same applies to governments: "God's ownership of the land is a limit on absolute ownership by anyone." Specifically, this means that "the government and the poor" are not "free to transgress God's laws regarding the same property." In sum: God's "commands do not allow for government redistribution of wealth." While it is true that the rich have a "responsibility to help the poor," the poor also "have a responsibility not to steal from the rich" (62–63). In sharp contrast to Rauschenbusch and Sider, Chilton gives us the ultimate antisocialist reading of Scripture: "The Bible stands against all forms of socialism and statism" (35). This sharp contrast should not let us lose sight of the important continuities among Rauschenbusch, Sider, and Chilton: All three thinkers find the answer to the query "What is the God-willed economic system?" directly in Scripture. While they validate their answers in different ways, formally they share a conviction that modern people's economic misery can only be relieved through a biblically ordered economy, however this is understood. There is a specific "biblical economy."

The sharp divergence among the three views we have now considered presents us with a challenge that is not unique to applying Scripture to economic life. The phenomenon of appealing to the same texts in Scripture to defend contradictory views is as old as the early church's conflict with Judaism and as recent as debates about homosexuality, the ordination of women, or creationism. There is no escape from the task of interpretation; we read and apply the Bible as fallible and finite human beings who will disagree with each other until our Lord returns. This is not a reason for despair or passivity; wrestling with the biblical text in Christian community and with the aid of the Holy Spirit is our lot and our privilege; it is at the core of what the apostle placed before us when he told the Philippian church and us to "work out your own salvation with fear and trembling" (Phil. 2:12). It is essential to recognize this inevitability and it reminds us that we all do this within the context of specific Christian traditions that guide us in our understanding of Scripture and help us avoid individualist and idiosyncratic interpretations. Our traditions, however, are not sacrosanct; we must always be open to being corrected by Scripture itself, an openness that includes honest listening to other traditions in order to be corrected if need be. With all this in mind, we turn now to an understanding of the relation between Scripture and economic life set forth in the Dutch Reformed tradition of neo-Calvinism by one of its two architects, Herman Bavinck.

With Bavinck we take a step back before moving forward; before we ask about his specific application of Scriptural teaching to economic life, we will ask whether this attempt is even appropriate; does the Bible intend to provide us with a normative economic system? We will see that Bavinck's own approach is *indirect*; the Bible's enduring *principles* need to be applied by mature and morally responsible Christian disciples in their worldly vocations.

Question 4: Is the very idea of looking for "a biblical economy" wrongheaded? Is there a better approach? What biblical themes are relevant for economics? Herman Bavinck and Biblical Principles

In his magisterial four-volume *Reformed Dogmatics*, Herman Bavinck (1845–1921) provided the theological muscle for the renaissance of Reformed thought and action in the late nineteenth century, famously represented by Abraham Kuyper and commonly referred to as neo-Calvinism. Bavinck's superb mind and fertile pen, however, were not restricted to purely doctrinal, theological topics. As he and other neo-Calvinists saw it, biblical truth was applicable to all of life. As challenging as the task of moving from ancient biblical text to contemporary issue might be, it was a challenge that had to be met. And Bavinck did. As Richard Mouw put it in his book jacket endorsement for Bavinck's translated collection of shorter writings, *Essays on Religion, Science, and Society*: "Here an amazing nineteenth-century Calvinist mind addresses with much wisdom a twentieth-first century agenda."

In 1891 Bavinck prepared a report for the First Christian Social Congress in Amsterdam with the title "General Biblical Principles and the Relevance of Concrete Mosaic Law for the Social Question Today." That is the same year Pope Leo XIII inaugurated a century and more of Roman Catholic social teaching with his encyclical *Rerum Novarum* ("On the Condition of Workers"). It is also the year that Abraham Kuyper gave his famous address to the same First Christian Social Congress in Amsterdam titled "The Social Question and the Christian Religion" (*Het Sociale Vraagstuk en de Christelijke Religie*), which James Skillen has translated and edited under the title *The Problem of Poverty*. There are striking parallels between the Roman Catholic and neo-Calvinist traditions of social teaching, notably the united opposition to socialism as the answer to the social crisis of the day. Neither Bavinck nor the pope shrinks back from the imperative of Christian obligation to those in need. Being a follower of Jesus Christ is incompatible with indifference to the misery and pain of poverty, destitution, disease, and hunger. Lazarus is at our door and the fires of hell await those who dismiss him while they party. Loving Jesus obligates his followers to care for the poor.

But how does this happen? How should it happen? How does the Bible guide us? Does the Bible instruct followers of Jesus on specific economic questions? Does our Lord's proclamation of the kingdom of God or his Nazareth sermon on Isaiah 61 ("The Spirit of the Lord is upon me, because he has anointed me to proclaim good news to the poor. . . ."; Luke 4:18) translate to concrete economic actions and institutions? Rauschenbusch and Sider concluded that it did and, furthermore, that it included some form of redistribution of wealth in order to lift up the needy and the poor. Without providing an explanation or justification, both men simply assume a direct move from Jesus' teaching to modern economic life.

Bavinck's Reformed alternative to such a direct move is not just a matter of exegesis or interpreting specific texts; it is a fundamental challenge to understanding the purpose of Scripture itself. What does the Bible intend to reveal to us? What are the appropriate questions to put to the Bible? If we do not, for example, ask the Bible if it is okay to drive cars or whether we should stick to horse-drawn carriages and buggies, whether we may use electricity instead of kerosene, take out insurance policies or mortgages, why should we inquire about a "biblical economics" for our modern world?

A Reformed approach to the Bible resists reading it in a flat manner as so many disparate bits and pieces of inspired, useful knowledge that can be picked up here and there as we have need of them. A Reformed handling of Scripture does not treat it as a manual for child rearing one day and a textbook for financial management the next. It is a mistake to go to the Bible for scientific knowledge, a point John Calvin already made in his *Genesis* commentary when he observed that the words "let there be a firmament" (1:6) are meant not for the sophisticated men of learning but "for all men without exception" and can be understood even by the "rude and unlearned." Calvin then added: "He who would learn astronomy, and other recondite arts, let him go elsewhere." Two important aspects of a Reformed hermeneutics are illustrated here: The first is the perspicuity of Scripture, the conviction arising from the priesthood of all believers that Scripture's essential message can be grasped by all who have been renewed by the Holy Spirit. Reformed people do not rely on a priestly caste of theologians to tell them how to read the Bible. Second, though the Bible is relevant for every dimension of human life, it has a very specific and well-defined purpose: "that by believing you may have life in his name" (John 20:31). The Bible is a *salvation* book and not an economics textbook or social renewal manual. And it is with this particular focus on salvation that Bavinck addresses the question of the Bible's relevance for economics.

Rauschenbusch and Sider and many who follow in their footsteps appeal to the New Testament and Jesus' eschatological teaching about the kingdom of God as the model for a radical new economic order. Bavinck rejects this out of hand; the message of the New Testament is primarily religious or spiritual. Jesus did not come into the world to improve social conditions.

ECONOMIC SHALOM | JOHN BOLT

Thus, according to Bavinck the first order of the day is restoring our proper relationship with God. The cross of Christ, therefore, is the heart and midpoint of the Christian religion. Jesus did not come, first of all, to renew families and reform society but to save sinners and to redeem the world from the coming wrath of God. This salvation of our souls must be our ultimate concern for which we are willing to sacrifice everything: father and mother, house and field, even our own lives, in order to inherit the kingdom of heaven (Matthew 6:33; 16:26) ("General Biblical Principles and the Relevance of Concrete Mosaic Law for the Social Question Today [1891]," 443).

Bavinck's dismissal of New Testament eschatology as a platform for social transformation runs directly against the grain of most contemporary interpreters of the Gospels. When people become dissatisfied with the church's failure to radically change the world, they usually rally to the emphasis on the kingdom of God. The church, it is then said, is not about "saving souls" but needs to "participate in God's mission of establishing the kingdom." A French Roman Catholic modernist, Alfred Loisy, is reported to have said, "Jesus proclaimed the kingdom of God, and what came was the church," with the obvious implication that something important was lost in the translation. When one explores the "About" section of the World Communion of Reformed Churches' Web site, one finds this action goal:

> WCRC coordinates joint church initiatives for economic, ecological and gender justice based on the member churches' common theology and beliefs.
>
> Our objectives are to foster unity among our member churches and promote economic, social and environmental justice.

In view of this strong trend, isn't thinking of the New Testament in essentially "spiritual" categories of "saving sinners" nothing less than an unfortunate return to a now-discredited version of Christianity that is "so heavenly minded it is no earthly good"?

Ironically, it is just the reverse. When the church trades in the bread of the gospel of forgiveness of sin and conversion to Jesus Christ as Savior and Lord for the stones of earthly transformation, she loses both. Bavinck insists that the world's problem, first of all, is not that there is injustice, poverty, and brokenness that needs to be fixed but that we are sinners, alienated from God and standing under judgment. To say that the mission of Jesus and the gospel message of the New Testament are "spiritual" is to point to the only way all social relationships and realities can be reconciled and healed. Bavinck puts it this way: "Redemption does not set aside the differences that exist thanks to God's will but renews all relationships to their original form by bringing all of them into a reconciled relationship with God" ("Resolution 3," in "General Biblical Principles," 445).

But what does this look like concretely? Where do we go to for guidance in how to live in those relationships as new creatures in Christ? Like theonomist David Chilton, Bavinck turns to the Old Testament Law of Moses for help. However, unlike Chilton, he does not take Mosaic law as such to be a blueprint by which we can govern modern society. Rather, Bavinck's vision goes back to creation itself and to the laws, ordinances, and institutions, that are universal for all people. Human life in society, including culture, political economy, social structures, and institutions, is not the product of redemption or biblical revelation but a given of creation, and its concrete manifestation is a gift of divine providence. Therefore, the redemption that we receive in Christ does not overthrow the laws, ordinances, and structures of creation. If we want to know how the world "works," we do not start with the gospel but with our life in creation. At the same time, we live in a world where sin mars, distorts, and even breaks all our relationships and places them under divine judgment.

To go to Old Testament law does not mean that the Mosaic Code is a blueprint for all societies but that it is *revelation* to God's covenant people illumining for them what God's will as Creator is for us. We learn biblical *principles* that point back to the order of creation itself. This results in claims that are more modest. Instead of speaking of a "biblical economics," or insisting that "Scripture demands" or "requires" this or that specific economic system or policy, Bavinck will only speak of a matter *being consistent with biblical teaching*, using language like "Therefore, it is entirely in keeping with Holy Scripture to . . ."

Bavinck concluded his address to the 1891 Social Congress with a series of seven resolutions derived from key biblical principles, including maintaining a civic sabbath day, preventing accumulation of capital and property, and ensuring, as much as possible, a "living wage" for every person. Whether or not one agrees with Bavinck on these specifics, it needs to be noted that he insists that there are necessary concrete consequences for social and economic policy that flow from these principles. This needs to be emphasized; scriptural teaching and Christian doctrine do need to be made concrete through application to actual situations and problems.

I want to conclude this chapter with a brief final theological assessment of the different viewpoints examined in this chapter and follow that with my own perspective.

Those who attempt to derive biblically based patterns for modern economic life appeal to different dimensions or themes in Christian theology. Rauschenbusch and Sider found their biblical resource in the *eschatology* of the New Testament, notably Jesus' teaching about the kingdom of God. An eschatological vision of the coming kingdom of God serves as the template for economic and social life today. Chilton and Bavinck appeal to Old Testament biblical law, with Bavinck emphasizing the point that Old Testament law is *revelation* about the laws, ordinances, structures, and institutions of *creation*. Old Testament Mosaic law reveals to us *principles* that illumine the divinely ordained patterns of creation itself. I fully agree with Bavinck that a Christian social ethic, including a normative understanding of our economic life, must be rooted in creation and not in eschatology. As I will discuss in chapter 4, a proper understanding of biblical eschatology should inform our social ethics, but as a check on perfectionist utopianism, not as a template for radical transformation of our social order. However, I believe that there are several additional valuable resources for economic life to be mined from scriptural teaching.

First, we do need to begin with the biblical doctrines of creation and providence. "The earth is the LORD's and the fullness thereof, the world and those who dwell therein . . ." (Ps. 24:1). Principles of stewardship and use of the earth's resources clearly flow from this confession. These need to be translated into concrete policy and law. But there is also another theological field that is implied in Bavinck's discussion, namely, *anthropology*. The freedom and dignity of the human person as the image of God has much to teach us about what we should look for in any economic system or policy, and we shall explore that further in the next chapter. Here we will not be looking for specific principles that are directly relevant for economics (laws about theft, private property, restitution, fair wages, etc.) but for perennial truths about human nature.

In addition, we must not overlook the Wisdom Literature of the Bible as an invaluable resource for these perennial truths. Wisdom Literature reflects the accumulated, tried-and-true insight about who we are, how we act, and how we should act. Many readers mistakenly treat biblical Wisdom Literature as though it were law or, worse, gospel. "Whoever spares the rod hates his son" (Prov. 13:24) then turns into a command ("Spare the rod and spoil the child"), and "Train up a child in the way he should go; even when he is old he will not depart from it" (Prov. 22:6) becomes a gospel promise. Biblical wisdom is descriptive and only indirectly prescriptive; it prudentially directs us to the *limits* and *boundaries* of our life in creation, boundaries we transgress at the expense of our happiness and flourishing in God's world and in community. The following passages from the Wisdom Literature of the Bible continue to instruct us:

"He who loves money will not be satisfied with money, nor he who loves wealth with his income; this also is vanity." (Eccl. 5:10)

"A greedy man stirs up strife, but the one who trusts in the LORD will be enriched." (Prov. 28:25)

"Whoever oppresses the poor to increase his own wealth, or gives to the rich, will only come to poverty." (Prov. 22:16)

"Whoever is generous to the poor lends to the LORD, and he will repay him for his deed." (Prov. 19:17)

"The rich rules over the poor, and the borrower is the slave of the lender." (Prov. 22:7)

"Remove far from me falsehood and lying; give me neither poverty nor riches; feed me with the food that is needful for me." (Prov. 30:8)

Along with key theological themes from the Christian doctrines of creation, anthropology, and eschatology, biblical wisdom offers the prudential guidance that we, as free Christian disciples led by the Holy Spirit, can apply to life in our modern economy. Christians also learn from the incarnation and example of Christ. The doctrine of the incarnation reminds us that in "becoming flesh and dwelling among us" God affirms and blesses materiality (see John 1:14). The example of Christ's life must be used with care.

On the one hand, Mary's Magnificat reminds us that in Christ's coming God "brought down the mighty from their thrones" and "exalted those of humble estate," "filled the hungry with good things," and "the rich he has sent away empty" (Luke 1:52–53). Furthermore, as noted earlier our Lord's first sermon in Nazareth has Isaiah 61 as its text: "The Spirit of the Lord is upon me . . . to proclaim good news to the poor. . . . to proclaim liberty to the captives and recovering of sight to the blind, to set at liberty those who are oppressed, and to proclaim the year of the Lord's favor" (Luke 4:18–19). But, we should also bear in mind the story of Zacchaeus (Luke 19) and the accusation against Jesus that, thanks to his eating and drinking with "tax collectors and sinners," he was a "a glutton and a drunkard" (Matt. 11:19). John Schneider gives us a balanced judgment when he says that "there was certainly a poverty about Jesus." However, he also warns against "overstating the economic lowliness attending his birth," as in his identification with the poor in his ministry. "For it is not that Christ in his earthly incarnation did not 'identify' with the poor; clearly he did. It is just that he also in quite different ways identified with people in other social and economic classes, too. Moreover, the language of being 'rich' and 'poor' in terms of Jesus' identification is semantically slippery" (*The Good of Affluence*, 124, 118).

A balanced approach to using the Bible to inform our economic life is multifaceted and includes illumination of creation principles, biblical wisdom, a biblical anthropology and eschatology, and the incarnation and example of Christ. This approach reflects a Reformed understanding of Scripture and also of human knowledge. Reformed people do not turn to the Bible for specific economic programs or policies, because they believe that these are given in God's order of creation; we must learn about the specifics of these laws by studying creation and human experience. At the same time, recognizing that our understanding of the world is also tainted by sin and needs special revelation, Reformed people also make use of what they learn from Scripture and use it to understand concrete human experience. Thus, informed about human nature (that it is created, fallen, and redeemed), and world history (that it is under divine judgment and grace) Reformed Christians form theories and propose policies that will do justice to biblical revelation. We should not say, therefore, that a particular system of economics is "*the* biblical system"; the best we can do is call attention to features that are consistent with or at odds with a biblical understanding of humanity and the world.

Discussion Questions

1. How do you use the Bible for guidance in the practical questions of daily living?

2. What biblical texts or passages about economics, work, or money are most important to you? Are there themes you tend to overlook or miss?

3. How do you understand and apply Jesus' teaching about the kingdom of God?

4. Reflecting on Matthew 11:19, one author, somewhat irreverently, referred to Jesus as a "party animal." More reverently, what is the relevance to our Christian walk of Jesus' example in "eating and drinking with tax collectors and sinners"?

5. Do you view the expression "social gospel" favorably or negatively?

For Further Reading

Bavinck, Herman. "General Biblical Principles and the Relevance of Concrete Mosaic Law for the Social Question Today (1891)." Translated by John Bolt. *Journal of Markets and Morality* 13, no. 2 (Fall 2010): 411–46. http://www.marketsandmorality.com/index.php/mandm/article/view/103/97.

Chilton, David. *Productive Christians in an Age of Guilt-Manipulators.* Tyler, TX: Institute for Christian Economics, 1981.

Kuyper, Abraham. *The Problem of Poverty.* Translated by James W. Skillen. Washington, DC: Center for Public Justice / Grand Rapids: Baker, 1991. Originally delivered as an address at the opening of the Social Congress on November 9, 1891 (Amsterdam, November 9–12, 1891) and then published that same year as *Het Sociale Vraagstuk en de Christelijke Religie* [The social question and the Christian religion].

Rauschenbusch, Walter. *Christianity and the Social Crisis.* New York: Macmillan, 1907.

———. *Christianizing the Social Order.* New York: MacMillan, 1912.

———. *The Righteousness of the Kingdom.* Edited by Max Stackhouse. Nashville: Abingdon, 1968.

Schneider, John R. *The Good of Affluence: Seeking God in a Culture of Wealth.* Grand Rapids: Eerdmans, 2002.

Sider, Ronald J. *Rich Christians in an Age of Hunger: A Biblical Study.* Nashville: Thomas Nelson, 2005. Originally published in 1977. Citations are to the 2005 edition.

Created for Creative Production | 2

Imago Dei and Human Vocation

Teach me, my God and King,
In all things thee to see,
And what I do in any thing,
To do it as for thee:

. . . .

A servant with this clause
Makes drudgerie divine:
Who sweeps a room, as for thy laws,
Makes that and th' action fine.

George Herbert, "The Elixir"

I n common usage, the two questions "What are you going to *be* when you grow up?" and "What are you going to *do* when you grow up?" are practically interchangeable. Yet, there is a significant difference between them. The second one is functional and utilitarian; implied in the question is another question: "What job are you going to accept in order to keep yourself alive?" The question is born out of practical realism: "There is no such thing

~ 25 ~

as a free lunch." The first one includes in it a notion of *vocation* or calling: "What identity do you envision for yourself? Do you see yourself as a doctor, an engineer, a missionary, a teacher . . . what?"

In a biblically normative understanding of work, the first question ought to be predominant. As we contemplate our calling, we will not simply consider the current job market ("today we need carpenters, tomorrow we will need computer programmers"), but ask ourselves first-order questions about who we are, why we are here, how God has gifted us, and how we can best serve his purposes. This is the ideal, and it is captured by George Herbert's line in the epigraph above about doing everything "as for thee" so that "Nothing can be so mean, / Which with his tincture (for thy sake) / Will not grow bright and clean."

But, as we know all too well, work is not always like that. Far too often and for far too many people, the character of work is captured by that wonderfully descriptive word "drudgery." This can be summed up by a phrase lifted out of context from a well-known Christmas carol—"far as the curse is found"—with "the curse" of course referring to Genesis 3:17–19. At best, our work is often ambiguous; we have some sense of what it is for, but it often seems less than truly fulfilling. In the words of the song "Heigh Ho" by lyricist Larry Morey, written for Disney's 1937 animated film *Snow White and the Seven Dwarves*:

> We dig dig dig dig dig dig dig in our mine the whole day through
> To dig dig dig dig dig dig dig is what we really like to do . . .
> But we don't know what we dig 'em for

Another song in this animated musical, "Just Whistle while You Work," symbolically captures one of the key escape strategies used by people whose work is less than fully satisfying.

> Just whistle while you work . . .

So hum a merry tune . . .
When hearts are high the time will fly so whistle while you work

Substitute internet surfing, or, tragically, alcohol and even drugs, for whistling, and we have a description of the work situation for far too many people. Now, it must be said that drudgery takes different forms, and today's drudgery is a far cry from the drudgery of those living in the nineteenth or sixteenth century, to say nothing of the centuries before Christ. Work in a windowless, Dilbert-like office cubicle, managing numbers on computer screens that appear unconnected from "real life," may seem like drudgery, but having central heating in the winter and air conditioning in the summer is a vast improvement over the conditions faced by serfs in the twelfth century, factory workers in the nineteenth, or coal miners in the twentieth. At the same time, we must never forget that for far too many people around the world, work, if it can be found, is truly drudgery.

We need not belabor the point; there is something not altogether right about our work. Work is all too often a means to another end rather than a satisfying end in itself. Work, says Dorothy Sayers in her wonderful essay "Why Work?" should be seen "not as a necessary drudgery to be undergone for the purpose of making money, but as a way of life in which the nature of man should find its proper exercise and delight and so fulfill itself to the glory of God. . . . [I]t should, in fact, be thought of as a creative activity undertaken for the love of the work itself; and that man, made in God's image, should make things, as God makes them, for the sake of doing well a thing that is well worth doing" (In *Letters to a Diminished Church: Passionate Arguments for the Relevance of Christian Doctrine*, 125). The basis for this vision is found in the biblical creation story in Genesis that describes God's creative acts over a six-day period, with a twofold climax. Humanity is the highpoint, the crown of creation, blessed and given royal authority over the rest of God's creatures:

> Then God said, "Let us make man in our image, after our likeness. And let them have dominion over the fish of the sea and over the birds of the heavens and over the livestock and over all the earth and over every creeping thing that creeps on the earth." (Gen. 1:26)

After the record states that God so created human beings, male and female, we are given a divine blessing and mandate:

> God blessed them. And God said to them, "Be fruitful and multiply and fill the earth and subdue it, and have dominion over the fish of the sea and over the birds of the heavens and over every living thing that moves on the earth." (Gen. 1:28)

Our calling as God's image bearers and vice-regents in creation is repeated: We are to be kings and queens in our work. We were created for creative production, including the wonderful and mysterious joining of a man and a woman to create new life.

We Americans are not fond of royal imagery; our very identity was forged in rebellion against royal tyranny. And, we must grant that the idea of ruling over creation runs a real risk of providing an excuse for exploitation and spoliation of the natural world. In spite of this, I believe that much of the unhappiness that people have with their work results from frustration over our royal status and role. Rather than masters over our work, we are its slaves; we don't rule over our work, it rules us. In the film *Modern Times*, Charlie Chaplin's comic routine of a frantic man on an assembly line is the perfect image of this. We work to make money to consume products that are made for the purpose of providing work. Our "stuff" rules us.

The Reformed tradition speaks of a threefold office for our

Lord and for his followers. The Heidelberg Catechism explains the name "Christ," or "anointed," with the offices of prophet, priest and king (Lord's Day 12). The follow-up question and answer describe Christian existence in the same terms. We are called "Christians," so the answer responds, "Because by faith I am a member of Christ and so I share in his anointing. I am anointed to confess his name, to present myself to him as a living sacrifice of thanks, to strive with a free conscience against sin and the devil in this life, and afterward to reign with Christ over all creation for eternity." But what did this kingly, royal office mean for humanity *before* the fall and the curse of Genesis 3? Let me suggest that, minimally, Adam and Eve's royal office implied dignity and freedom for creative production; for using the manifold riches of creation to enhance human flourishing.

I say "minimally" because the Genesis creation story itself, and especially the commentary on it by the rest of Scripture, makes it clear that there is more. Above everything else we *are* image bearers of God. Every human person has a dignity and worth that is separable from what he or she can do or actually does. Those who, because of disease, disability, or weakness cannot do what the able-bodied are capable of doing, are no less divine image bearers. Nowhere does this become clearer than in the perspective provided by comparing the first Adam's status and role with those of Christ, the Second Adam. The apostle Paul draws the comparison in 1 Corinthians 15 between the "natural, earthly, living being" Adam and the "spiritual, heavenly, life-giving" Christ. This description, we must emphasize, refers to the prefall Adam. What the Second Adam gained for us was more than what the first one lost. What is implied here is that we were created for something more than what the first humans possessed. What that was is hinted at by the writer to the Hebrews who, speaking of Christ's superiority over the angels, notes that "it was not to angels that God subjected the world to come" (Heb. 2:5). He warrants this by an appeal to Psalm 8 and its exaltation of humans as God's vice-regents:

> What is man, that you are mindful of him,
>   or the son of man, that you care for him?
> You made him for a little while lower than the angels;
>   you have crowned him with glory and honor,
>   putting everything in subjection under his feet.
>   (Heb. 2:6–8)

We were created to rule over creation now and destined for even greater ruling in eternity.

To understand this added dimension we need to consider the second and real climax to the creation story in Genesis 1— the Sabbath. Created to image God, humans follow God in his working on the six days of creation. But, God rested on the seventh day, and Scripture makes it clear that humans are to follow suit. The Exodus version of the fourth commandment explicitly makes the connection: "For in six days the LORD made heaven and earth, the sea, and all that is in them, and rested on the seventh day. Therefore the LORD blessed the Sabbath day and made it holy" (Exod. 20:11). Once again, the writer to the Hebrews points to the eschatological sabbath "plus." After citing Genesis 2:2 ("And God rested on the seventh day from all his works"; Heb. 4:4), the author admonishes his readers to "strive to enter that rest" which remains (Heb. 4:11). But just before this, the writer says, "So then, there remains a Sabbath rest for the people of God, for whoever has entered God's rest has also rested from his works as God did from his" (Heb. 2:9–10). David Van Drunen's summary captures well the point I am trying to make:

> The first Adam did not bear God's image in order to work
> aimlessly in the original creation but to finish his work in
> this world and then to enter a new creation and to sit down

enthroned in royal rest. . . . He was not only to be like God
in exercising royal dominion in the original creation, but was
to enter into royal rest as ruler of the new creation, (*Living in
God's Two Kingdoms*, 40–41)

The Reformed tradition, we just noted, speaks of a threefold office for our Lord and also for his followers. We have been speaking of the royal or kingly office but now need to consider the office
of priest. Priests are those who serve in the presence of God; they
minister in the temple. In recent years, biblical scholars have increasingly pointed to the way in which the Genesis account of creation resembles the architecture and function of a temple building.
The building of Israel's tabernacle (Exod. 25–31) reflects the cosmic order of creation by using the sixfold pattern of God speaking
("The LORD said to Moses . . . ; 25:1; 30:11, 17, 22, 34; 31:1), followed by a command to keep the Sabbath (31:12). After the tabernacle construction is "completed" (39:12), the same Hebrew word
is used as in Genesis 2:2 to describe the completion of God's work.
Furthermore, this sevenfold pattern (time to build, feasts of dedication) is also used to describe the building of Solomon's temple
in 1 Kings 8 and 2 Chronicles 6–7. Creation itself is God's temple,
and the Jerusalem temple on Mount Zion is a microcosm of God's
creation temple:

> He chose the tribe of Judah,
>   Mount Zion, which he loves.
> He built his sanctuary like the high heavens,
>   like the earth, which he has founded forever.
>   (Ps. 78:68–69)

In the words of Peter Enns, "The creation story was written with
Israel's temple and the Sabbath rhythm in mind" (*The Evolution of
Adam*, 73). A summary of what we are setting forth here is cap-
tured in the biblical notion of a *royal priesthood*. This is how God

characterizes the vocation to which he calls his people in the Old Covenant as well as the New, as these two passages teach:

> You yourselves have seen what I did to the Egyptians, and how I bore you on eagles' wings and brought you to myself. Now therefore, if you will indeed obey my voice and keep my covenant, you shall be my treasured possession among all peoples, for all the earth is mine; and you shall be to me a kingdom of priests and a holy nation. (Exod. 19:4–6)

> But you are a chosen race, a royal priesthood, a holy nation, a people for his own possession, that you may proclaim the excellencies of him who called you out of darkness into his marvelous light. Once you were not a people, but now you are God's people; once you had not received mercy, but now you have received mercy. (1 Peter 2:9–10)

Why is this important? First, our work is performed *in the presence of God*. That is what gives it its significance, its meaning, its glory. Work must be done, primarily, for its own sake. Sayers once again provides us with wisdom: "We should ask of an enterprise, not 'will it pay?' but 'is it good?'; of a man, not 'what does he make?' but 'what is his work worth?'; of goods, not 'can we induce people to buy them?' but 'are they useful things well made?'; of employment, not 'how much a week?' but 'will it exercise my faculties to the utmost?'" ("Why Work?" in *Letters to a Diminished Church*, 132–33). This means, finally, that "work is not, primarily, a thing one does to live, but the thing one lives to do" (134–35). It also means that "the worker's first duty is to *serve the work*," i.e., to do it well (142). This is the proper way to give work the dignity it deserves. "[A worker] must be able to serve God *in* his work, and the work itself must be accepted and respected as the medium of divine creation." Sayers adds some advice for the church: "It is the business of the Church to recognize that the secular vocation, as such, is sacred. . . . [The Church] must concern Herself with seeing that the work itself is such as a human being can perform without degradation—that no one is required by economic or any other considerations to devote himself to work that is contemptible, soul destroying, or harmful" (138).

Second, there is more to human flourishing than work. Work is important but work isn't everything. Both Adam and we were created for more than just work; we were created for Sabbath, for eternity in the presence of God. This provides the necessary perspective on work that keeps us from the errors that frustrate us and inhibit human flourishing.

Perhaps the most prevalent error for readers of this volume will be the idolatry of work. Does your work define you? Does it stand in the way of important personal relationships with a spouse, children, family members, or fellow Christians? We are hardwired as God's image bearers to enjoy and find satisfaction and fulfillment in creative production. A carpenter who finishes a house, an entrepreneur who succeeds in a start-up, a professor who has mentored a graduate student, a pianist who has mastered a Beethoven sonata, a parent whose high school graduating son or daughter chooses to enter a profession where gifts will be used to honor Christ and glorify God—all of these (and the list could go on ad infinitum) are the fruit of human work, of using our hearts, minds, wills, and hands to fashion something that in its own way was raw, unformed, and capable of being fashioned. It is when we do such things that we image our Creator; we cooperate with the Holy Spirit in divine providence itself. This is glorious and wonderful, but also a temptation to pride. ("*My* child was the honor student . . ."; "See what *my* hands have done; see the mighty X that *I* have built." Cf. Dan. 4:30.)

The idolatry of work can also take the form of anxiety; it can be a failure of trust in God's providential care. When we feel that it is all up to us to provide for ourselves and our family; that our future security entirely depends on our own work and effort, on the accumulation of our retirement portfolios and careful investments, then Sabbath rest is also impossible. We are too busy working 24/7 to permit ourselves the leisure of Sabbath rest.

The perspective of royal priesthood, of work and service in the temple of God, before his face, provides the needed corrective. Our work is important but it does not save us. To introduce another theological notion, we are not *justified* by our *achievements*. This does not mean that we should jettison all notions of achievement. Of course not! Rather, it means, says Hans Küng, that a believer is "liberated from the obsessional neurosis of having to justify himself by his achievements." His summary, in the introduction of his book comparing the doctrine of justification in the theology of Karl Barth and the Roman Catholic Council of Trent, captures this well: "Because of his believing trust in the wholly Other, he knows that his life under all circumstances has a meaning: not only in successes, but also in failures; not only in brilliant achievements, but also in lapses; not only in increasing achievement, but also in declining achievement; not only in happiness, but also in unhappiness; not only in living, but also in dying" ("Justification Today" in *Justification*, liv–lv).

To think of our work as the work of a royal priest ennobles it, giving work a glory that comes from seeing it *sub specie aeternitatis* (from the vantage point of eternity).

Seeing our work from the perspective of eternity also leads us to confront the purely utilitarian understanding of work. One of the most perverse work slogans in human history was placed over some of the Nazi extermination camps, notably Auschwitz: *Arbeit macht frei* (labor makes [one] free). Yet, work done just so we can be free—for weekends, for holidays, for vacations, for leisure— undoubtedly reflects the mentality of many workers today. Our work is a necessary means to an end; our sense of flourishing is found only in the end and not in the means itself. In a broken

INTERLUDE 2

To work or not to work.

Not all people in our society make work an idol. Not all cultivate and maintain the habits that likely characterize most readers of this volume and tempt us to become workaholics. There are significant pockets of people in our society who do not participate in the work-force at all. Some, because of circumstances beyond their control, are unable to find employment. Some are so discouraged they have stopped looking. Others, however, choose to continue in dependence on state welfare rather than actively seeking work. Our workforce participation is reaching record lows while we continue to spend re-cord amounts consuming entertainment. Our society is a mixed bag that includes those shirking employment as well as workaholics. Both postures sin against the royal priesthood inherent in being an image bearer of God.

world, where we do not control all the circumstances of our lives, it does happen that many of us feel we have to "settle for less" than our preferred or optimal work. Whether they are all true or not, there are enough stories circulating of PhDs in philosophy and French literature working at McDonald's or Walmart, or driving taxicabs for their livelihood, to remind us that we can't always get what we desire. But speaking normatively, Christians should think of their work in terms of *vocations*, callings to serve God as royal priests.

We will consider the implications of all of this for public policy in subsequent chapters and note here only the important norm of liberty as the essential condition for us to serve our Lord as royal priests. The dignity of our work requires a civic polity that nurtures and supports the liberty and responsibility of moral agents. All forms of indenture and dependency militate against such dignity and thus frustrate human flourishing.

Perhaps, a perceptive reader will ask, "This exalted perspective and soaring rhetoric is all well and good, but aren't you forgetting 'the curse' of Genesis 3:17–19? All this sounds far too romantic and not at all realistic." To add to the problem, the author is a theologian and not a "worker" in the sense that sociologists speak of as from "the working class," but an "intellectual." Fair enough; I do not build houses or fix cars, drive a truck, pick up garbage, or change seniors' diapers in a nursing home; my work involves, among other things, reading books, talking to students, and writing. And since I love to do all these things, to be paid a salary for it is a double bonus. I know that in loving my work I am privileged. But everything I have written above applies to me, including the sins of idolizing my work or the temptation to treat it as a means to an end (let's say, an academic reputation). The portrait provided above is as "realistic" as the message of the gospel itself. Yes, the world is under a curse; but—thanks be to God!—in Christ we are a new creation and live in hope, a hope that will not leave us ashamed. There is hope for our work also.

And to this, we must add that perspective and attitude do make a difference. Consider the following often repeated story about three men hard at work with sledgehammers, breaking big rocks into smaller ones. "Asked what they were doing, the first answered, 'Making little rocks out of big ones.' The second replied, 'Making a living.' And the third said, 'Building a cathedral'" (John Julian Ryan, "Humanistic Work: Its Philosophical and Cultural Implications," in *A Matter of Dignity: Inquiries into the Humanization of Work*, 11). The backbreaking, repetitive, hard work is the same for all three, but the third man comes as close as possible to the normative portrait sketched in this chapter. My favorite image of someone whose attitude toward work captures this ideal is Alexander Solzhenitsyn's character Ivan Denisovich as portrayed by Tom Courtenay in the Caspar Wrede film adaptation (1970) of the novel *One Day in the Life of Ivan Denisovich*. Scene after scene after scene of dehumanizing drudgery, deprivation, and brutality in the cold Siberian prison camp prepares us for a long march of prisoners outside in subzero weather (-30° to -40°F) to a work site, apparently in the middle of nowhere, to build stone-block walls whose purpose is quite unclear. At the end of the day, when all the men head back to the camp, at the risk of missing roll call and being placed in solitary for ten days, Ivan stays behind to finish up the last bit of mortar and set the last stones in place. And then— my favorite scene—he carefully sights down one wall and then the other before leaving. Pride in work being done well, even meaningless work and even in those circumstances—that's dignity.

But let us not shy away from realism and briefly consider three realistic temptations and sins that beset our work.

1. Laziness and sloth. Work is demanding; it requires training, dedication, and perseverance. Here biblical wisdom is our guide and needs no additional commentary:

   In all toil there is profit, but mere talk tends only to poverty. (Prov. 14:23)

   Whoever works his land will have plenty of bread, but he who follows worthless pursuits will have plenty of poverty. (Prov. 28:19)

   For even when we were with you, we would give you this command: If anyone is not willing to work, let him not eat. (2 Thess. 3:10)

2. Failure adequately to compensate those who work for us.

   You shall not oppress your neighbor or rob him. The wages of a hired worker shall not remain with you all night until the morning. (Lev. 19:13)

   For the Scripture says, "You shall not muzzle an ox when it treads out the grain," and, "The laborer deserves his wages." (1 Tim. 5:18)

3. When our work makes us rich.

> He who loves money will not be satisfied with money, nor he who loves wealth with his income; this also is vanity. (Eccl. 5:10)

> No one can serve two masters, for either he will hate the one and love the other, or he will be devoted to the one and despise the other. You cannot serve God and money. (Matt. 6:24)

> Do not work for the food that perishes, but for the food that endures to eternal life, which the Son of Man will give to you. For on him God the Father has set his seal. (John 6:27)

And then, finally, this perspective that covers it all:

> For we brought nothing into the world, and we cannot take anything out of the world. But if we have food and clothing, with these we will be content. But those who desire to be rich fall into temptation, into a snare, into many senseless and harmful desires that plunge people into ruin and destruction. For the love of money is a root of all kinds of evils. It is through this craving that some have wandered away from the faith and pierced themselves with many pangs. (1 Tim. 6:7–10)

We would fail to be honest in our realism if we said nothing about those who want to work but, for whatever reason, cannot. This includes able-bodied people who remain chronically unemployed, those with severe disabilities, and those who are injured or infirm. In addition to Christian compassion and aid, our obligation to "the least of these" should lead us to look for structural and institutional ways to provide redress to their situation. As we do that, it is important to remind ourselves and others that our identity, dignity, and worth as image bearers of God are not determined by our work, our productivity, or our achievements. In a Christian worldview, *being* precedes *doing*; we *are* created in the image of God, and the joy of our work is found in the service of the One who made us and whose image we bear.

Dorothy Sayers concludes her thoughts on why we should work with this summation of the church's task: "If work is to find its right place in the world, it is the duty of the Church to see to it that the work serves God, and that the worker serves the work" ("Why Work?" 146). Amen!

Discussion Questions

1. Does your work satisfy you? Try to identify the reasons why or why not. What are the satisfying aspects and which aspects frustrate you?

2. Do you think of your work as
   a. a place to which you go?
   b. a sacred vocation in which you are serving God?
   c. an unfortunate necessity?
   d. a means to an end (money, leisure time, etc.)?
   e. something from which to retire as soon as you can afford it?
   f. other?

3. Did you choose your work more or less freely (i.e., without external coercion)?

4. Which of the Bible texts quoted in this chapter spoke most directly to you?

For Further Reading

Enns, Peter. *The Evolution of Adam: What the Bible Does and Does Not Say about Human Origins.* Grand Rapids: Brazos, 2012). See chapter 4, "Israel and Primordial Time," especially the section titled "Creation and Sanctuary," 70–73.

Küng, Hans. "Justification Today: An Introductory Chapter to the New Edition" (1980), translated by Edward Quinn. In *Justification: The Doctrine of Karl Barth and a Catholic Reflection*. Translated by Thomas Collins, Edmund E. Tolk, and David Granskou. Philadelphia: Westminster Press, 1981. First published in English in 1964.

Ryan, John Julian. "Humanistic Work: Its Philosophical and Cultural Implications." In *A Matter of Dignity: Inquiries into the Humanization of Work*. Edited by W. J. Heisler and John W. Houck. Notre Dame, IN: University of Notre Dame Press, 1977.

Sayers, Dorothy. "Why Work?" In *Letters to a Diminished Church: Passionate Arguments for the Relevance of Christian Doctrine*, 125–46. Nashville: W Pubishing Group, 2004. A compact and practical homily on the dignity of work, originally delivered on April 23, 1942, a time of great scarcity and conflict during World War II.

Van Drunen, David. *Living in God's Two Kingdoms: A Biblical Vision for Christianity and Culture*. Wheaton: Crossway, 2010. A practical and realistic approach to Christian discipleship in culture and society. Includes a helpful and clear analysis of the Genesis story of creation and fall in broader biblical perspective.

"It Takes a Village"? | 3

Flourishing Life in Society

A Christian society is not going to arrive until most of us really want it: and we are not going to want it until we become fully Christian. . . . I cannot learn to love my neighbour as myself till I learn to love God: and I cannot learn to love God except by learning to obey Him.

C. S. Lewis

Despotism, which in its nature is fearful, sees the most certain guarantee of its own duration in the isolation of men, and it ordinarily puts all its care into isolating them. There is no vice of the human heart that agrees with it as much as selfishness: A despot readily pardons the governed for not loving him, provided that they do not love each other.

Alexis de Tocqueville

Our reflections on work in the previous chapter were incomplete. We do not work as solitary individuals in isolation but always as participants in an economy, a social order involving, among other things, markets, contracts, and wages or salaries. All we said in our first chapter about the problems in speaking of a "biblical economy" is compounded when we try to sketch a normative view of society as a whole. For starters, the Bible knows nothing of what we call "society." "Society" is a theoretical abstraction taking the sum total of a myriad of associations and institutions, many of which themselves have no counterparts in Scripture. The Bible addresses fathers, mothers, and children, kings and subjects, masters and servants, and even peoples and nations, but offers no overarching sociology within which each of the specific players in a society all find their place. "Society" is a modern theoretical construct.

However, since our concern is with a view of society that contributes to human flourishing, we can provide a portrait that comports with a biblical understanding of the human person, created in God's image and living in God's world. When we return to the biblical creation story we discover a fascinating and initially jarring narrative note in Genesis 2:18. In Genesis 1, beginning with day three, after each of God's creative acts we read "And God saw that it was good." Furthermore, after the general description of God creating human beings, blessing them, and giving them a mandate to fill the earth and have dominion over it (Gen. 1:26–30), we read a broad and intensified affirmation: "And God saw everything that he had made, and *behold*, it was *very* good" (Gen. 1:31, emphasis added). Then comes the cold shower in Genesis 2:18: "Then the LORD God said, "*It is not good* that the man should be alone; I will make a helper fit for him" (emphasis added). The story of Eve's creation (in Hebrew, *ishah*, or *wo-man* in English, created from *ish* = man) follows, along with the command and blessing of verse 24: "Therefore a man shall leave his father and his mother and hold fast to his wife, and they shall become one flesh."

"It is not good that the man should be alone." For us to understand this properly, we must set aside for the moment modern notions of companionship marriage. The point is *not* that Adam was *lonely*; rather, there is something humanly *incomplete* about him. If humanity is to image God as the Creator intended, "man" needs the complement of "woman." Here we have, *in nuce*, the foundation of all social order.

"I will make a helper fit for him." Here, older translations such as "help meet" (KJV) or "helpmate" mislead us into thinking that what is suggested here is something like "assistant" or some kind of subordinate servant. The Hebrew word used here— *ezer*—in fact connotes strength and power. In the Old Testament, the term is most often used of God and often in parallelism with words or images that clearly denote strength and power as in the following passages (emphasis added):

> There is none like God, O Jeshurun,
>> who rides through the heavens to your *help*,
>> through the skies in his majesty. (Deut. 33:26)

> Happy are you, O Israel! Who is like you,
>> a people saved by the LORD,
> the shield of your *help*,
>> and the sword of your triumph! (Deut. 33:29)

Genesis 2:18 is thus best taken as an affirmation of the complementary *royal* dignity of the man and the woman. What this means for sex roles and a whole host of other social questions is beyond the concern of this chapter and volume. We are interested here only in the broader question of social order in general. How do social orders get formed, and how do they flow from or relate to this primal created structure of man and woman in complementary unity? In addition, what does this all imply for our work, for our social economies? What does it mean that the royal dignity and priestly service of working in the garden before the face of God is a *shared* office, not just an individual one?

The first implication seems so obvious as to be almost trite. Aside from the rare instance of a solitary and self-sufficient hermit, work is always social; we work for others, with others, and to benefit others. We are able to work because social, political, and economic structures are in place to provide opportunities for us to work. There is a grain of truth in the otherwise discredited slogan from the 2012 US presidential campaign, "If you've got a business—you didn't build that. Somebody else made that happen." Unlike bees, we are not born as natural workers. To become workers, children need to be given responsibilities (chores), become familiar with positive and negative consequences, and learn essential attitudes and habits along with basic skills. All of these are learned primarily in the family. And thus we return full circle to Genesis 2:18 and 1:31. A flourishing human society requires good citizens and willing, productive workers, and both are nurtured in healthy, flourishing families.

We need to look more closely at the intrinsic connection between marriage and family, particularly because the traditional understanding of family faces major challenges today. The portrait I will be sketching borrows heavily from Herman Bavinck's *The Christian Family*, recently published in English translation.[1] On the basis of Genesis 2, Bavinck affirms marriage as a comprehensive two-in-one-flesh union of a man and a woman, committed to a permanent and exclusive union for having and rearing children. In Bavinck's words, "God made two out of one, so that he could then make the two into one, one soul and one flesh. This kind of fellowship is possible only between two. From the very beginning, marriage was and is by virtue of its essential nature monogamous, an essential bond between one man and one woman, and therefore also a lifelong covenant" (*The Christian Family*, 7). The creation-based view of marriage leads to its fulfillment and expansion in the family. Family life is based on marriage, and flourishing family life requires healthy marriages that are attentive to

---

1   For the summary that follows, I am indebted to a review of Herman Bavinck's *The Christian Family* by my dear friend and brother in Christ Eduardo J. Echeverria, professor of philosophy at Sacred Heart Major Seminary, Detroit, Michigan. The review was published in the *Journal of Markets and Morality* 16, no. 1 (Spring 2013): 219–37 and is used by permission.

the Creator's intentions and order. As Bavinck explains, "Upon this fellowship of love, then, God has bestowed his blessing in a special way. He is the Creator of man and of woman, the Inaugurator of marriage, and the Sanctifier of matrimony. Each child born is the fruit of fellowship, and as such is also the fruit of divine blessing. The two-in-oneness of husband and wife expands with a child into a three-in-oneness" (7–8).

The connection between the man-woman union and the child is *organic* and, according to Bavinck, is the basis of human flourishing in broader social relationships. It is with the family that we develop our full humanity. "A person's becoming [integrally] human occurs within the home; here the foundation is laid for the forming of the future man and woman, of the future father and mother, of the future member of society, of the future citizen, of the future subject in the kingdom of God" (108). The nurture that takes place in the family is irreplaceable; nothing can substitute for it:

> The family does not consist of a number of empty forms that we need to fill, but it is full of life. The husband and wife, coming from differing families, each contributes their own genetic makeup, tradition, nature, character, disposition, and life. And each child born to them is a member of humanity, a person with capacities like those of everyone else, and yet distinguished from all those others, whose relation is close or distant, with a unique existence and character. . . .
>
> Therefore the nurture that takes place within the family possesses a very special character. (106–7)

The moral health of families, therefore, is of "extraordinary significance" for flourishing life in human society. "For there in the family from the moment we enter the world we get to know all those relationships that we will enter later in society—relationships of freedom and connectedness, independence and dependence, authority and obedience, equality and difference." Bavinck adds:

"In the family we get to know the secret of life, the secret, namely, that not selfishness but self-denial and self-sacrifice, dedication and love, constitute the rich content of human living. And from the family we carry those moral relationships into society" (134).

But exactly *how* does this happen? How do we move organically from *man + woman* ⇒ *child = family* to agriculture, animal husbandry, trade and commerce, and city building? Consider a man and woman who have two sons. The elder becomes a field farmer who tills the ground and harvests its produce. The younger becomes a shepherd and domesticates animals. We can imagine the future of the two brothers and their offspring—provided they get along and one doesn't kill the other!—supplying resources for each other and each other's clan. The grain producer's crops are milled by a second party who then sells the flour for the village's bread bakers. Similarly, the domestication of animals yields milk, meat, wool, and hides for the village. To make this all work, however, we need more. As communities grow and differentiate, relationships become more complex. Simple barter exchanges between two people no longer suffice. Eventually some form of a market and a standard medium of exchange becomes necessary. In addition—because we do know about the reality of sinful human nature—the field farmer needs to be able to protect his crops from plunder and the animal farmer his flocks and herds from rustlers. Both, therefore, need land security or a nascent right of property. The village requires an agreed-upon rule of law. We will not pursue this any further here, saving a more extensive discussion of markets for chapter 5.

Our concern in this chapter is with the way social orders come into existence, and the case we are putting forth is that they arise *organically* and *spontaneously* from the primal, creation-grounded institutions of marriage and family. Honesty here requires me to acknowledge that this is a disputable. The portrait we have sketched comes with an acknowledgement of ignorance. While we might have some understanding of the myriad of individual associations in a social order, such as barter and association for protection against a common enemy, we simply do not know how the whole came together into the social order that is now our inescapable context. Furthermore, we cannot know it; it is beyond the capacity of a single person and eludes any single comprehensive explanation. This is what we mean when we speak of *organic* and *spontaneous* order; it was not planned in advance or constructed by human design.

As we said, this is a disputable claim, and we need to contrast it with the alternative, the conviction that social orders are *constructed* with a certain degree of intelligent intention or design and that careful analysis can deconstruct that intention. Thus, the currently fashionable "isms" of social analysis—racism, sexism, classism—are proposed as *explanations* by *unmasking* the present order of things and providing tools to effect social change. In this instance, as economist Friedrich Hayek explained, society is considered as an *organization* displaying "[the kind of] order which is achieved by *arranging* the relations between the parts according to a preconceived plan" ("Kinds of Order in Society," *New Individualist Review* 3, no. 2 (1964), repr. in *The Politicization of Society*, 506). Among the influential social and political thinkers who held variants of this view, we can include Jean-Jacques Rousseau and Karl Marx.

Mentioning Rousseau and Marx underscores the fact that the alternative to the view we are advocating in this chapter arises from dissatisfaction with the existing social order. Thus Rousseau begins his important treatise *Social Contract* with these famous words: "Man was born free, and he is everywhere in chains." Rather than seeing social institutions as the organic or spontaneous development of cumulative human actions rooted in human nature, Rousseau saw them as artificial vehicles of oppression. A similar sentiment is found in Marx's famous maxim, "The philosophers have only interpreted the world, in various ways: the point, however, is to change it." We do not have the space here to explore this alternative understanding of society in any detail but will summarize it by briefly considering three key notions in this worldview, *ideology*, *alienation*, and *liberation*.

Ideologues see society through the lenses of privileged insight that unmask what Kenneth Minogue has aptly called hidden "alien powers" behind such oppressive social realities as racism, sexism (including heterosexism and homophobism), classism, militarism, imperialism, and capitalism, not to mention specieism (the belief that humans are superior to animals). Since these alien powers have metaphysical status—though they cannot be empirically identified or measured; nor can one ever know if and when they are defeated—the ultimate historical struggle is not, as Christians believe, between the City of God and the Earthly City, but between oppressors and oppressed, exploiters and exploited. In Professor Minogue's words, "ideology is the conviction that current societies are cleverly concealed forms of dehumanizing oppression" (*Alien Powers: The Pure Theory of Ideology*, xviii). The list of oppressors and exploiters includes males, imperialists, the white race, the worldwide Jewish conspiracy, banks, and international corporations.

The Marxist notion of alienation is closely linked to all this; human beings are themselves the creators of the alien powers that enslave them, and ignorance of this is *false consciousness*. For Marx, man is defined by his capacity for creative action, for production—he is *homo faber*. This includes the creation of social structures and institutions that begin in human imagination and are then erected in reality. When we confuse these creations of our imagination with human reality itself, we have become alienated from our true, social selves. We need, therefore, to be liberated from alienating and oppressive structures—religion, marriage and family, tribe and nation, and even the state—in order to return to our true human, social being. Marx does not mean by this the positive, concrete social relationships in which we find ourselves but *universal humanity*, which Marx refers to as *species life*. We are truly emancipated when we become free from *particular* social relationships and see ourselves as part of a great human whole. In the words of a *Peanuts* character: "I love mankind . . . It's *people* I can't stand!!"

The real difference between the two views I am sketching can be seen via two metaphors. What I will call the "constructivist" view reminds us of how engineers work. It thinks that society, "the contingent world we actually inhabit, with all its unpredictabilities, was actually a system. Systems are sets of mechanisms that work in scientifically explicable ways. . . . To follow through the logic of such systems was to imagine that the social opacity of the human world had turned into a transparent drama, or more generally melodrama, in which the good could reliably be distinguished from the bad" (Minogue, *Alien Powers*, xix).

The organic and spontaneous order view, by contrast, looks like a crystal. "We could never produce a crystal by directly placing [i.e., *mechanically*] the individual molecules from which it is built up. But we can create the conditions under which such a crystal will form itself. . . . Similarly, we can create the conditions under which a biological organism will grow and develop" (507–8). We know in part, but the process of the whole eludes us. The most obvious example of such organic development in the social world is language itself. We can abstract from concrete language certain general rules that are universal, and we may even be able to trace the historical evolution of specific languages and how languages relate one to another, but the actual formation of a language is a form of organic and spontaneous order, not an engineered or arranged one. Furthermore, attempts to engineer a universal language like Esperanto have not lived up to their own hype (for example, bringing about world peace). The Tower of Babel, so Christians believe, has already been reversed—at Pentecost!

In arguing against claims of ideologists to have comprehensive knowledge of society's power structures, there are two important points that proponents of the organic view need to make. First, we do not deny the harsh realities of our world, including the presence of racism, sexism, classism, and militarism. Furthermore, we deplore the way in which racial bias, discrimination against women, and prejudice against those who did not grow up in the "right neighborhoods" and go to the "right schools" often shape conduct. We are committed to a society where people "will not be judged by the color of their skin but by the content of their character." We also believe in open and free societies where there is equality of opportunity. At the same time, we are also skeptical that social orders can be coerced into eliminating these and similar sins. This requires changed hearts, and, even then, we are realists about the prospects of eliminating sin and the pain caused by sin before our Lord's return. Second, we are capable of understanding key components of our social, economic, and political order, and therefore have *some* idea how people respond to incentives and disincentives. Believing that social orders come into being does not preclude us from judicious adjustments of parts of that order, always mindful that because of our limited knowledge we need to be open to self-correction. A preference for "organic" responses to evils does not mean quietism and inaction; it means cautious and limited reaction and an aversion to grand social scheming.

We are speaking of the *social order* here, that complex, connected web of relationships that includes our families, our work, our buying and selling, our involvement in churches, schools, clubs, and our leisure, along with the myriad means of communication. Perhaps, nothing underscores the truth of a spontaneous order interpretation so clearly as the last-mentioned global reality of twenty-first-century communication structure—the world of cybernetics, including computers, artificial intelligence, the internet, the "cloud," cell towers, smart phones, and so forth. This

"world" was not designed or planned; a series of smaller technological advances spontaneously came together, in fits and starts,
to produce it.

If we reject the idea that we can realize a whole new utopian
vision of the world by the sheer will of planners and organizers, we
do need another perspective on rational human action for addressing the flaws in our social orders. In a *Journal of Markets and Morality* article titled "Spontaneous Order versus Organized Order," Jan
Klos notes that the French Christian social thinker Frédéric Bastiat (1801–50) explained this need in terms of *responsibility* and
solidarity. Human beings created in the image of God are rational
and willful; we are responsible for our actions and must live with
the consequences. That responsibility includes a *spontaneous* following of our conscience and living with the consequences of failing to do so. We must also act in accord with our natures and the
natural order. At the same time, we are also sinful human beings
and need sanctions against our evil inclinations. Bastiat speaks of
"three sanctions that enforce the law of responsibility": (1) natural sanction, (2) religious sanction, and (3) legal sanction (169). In
all three, the key is reinforcing the awareness that our *actions have
consequences*. And it is here that Bastiat speaks of *solidarity*. We
humans are not atoms or self-sufficient entities. Our actions have
consequences for others. This too does not need to be imposed on
us by the state or utopian ideology; it arises naturally from the
family and the associations and allegiances that flow from it.

One possible objection to this view of social order might be
the polity of the United States of America itself. Is America not a
nation founded upon an idea, the idea that "all men are created
equal, that they are endowed by their Creator with certain un-
alienable Rights, that among these are Life, Liberty and the pursuit of Happiness" (*The Declaration of Independence*)? Well, yes and
no. Clearly, the founders "constructed" a polity founded on a set of
ideas or convictions, perhaps better described as a *creed*. However,

this creed had a long pedigree; it was not a utopian vision but rested on the insights of experience in governance and polity going back to the Greeks and Romans and was permeated with biblical wisdom about human nature. Furthermore, the founders sought to provide the frame for an experiment in ordered liberty, not a coerced utopia. This polity not only left room for a rich spontaneous associational life, it encouraged it by restricting the power of the federal state and devolving it downward to the states and local communities in the Tenth Amendment of the Bill of Rights to the US Constitution.

Let us conclude by asking about the conditions that make for human flourishing in society. At the individual and "part" level, we can make it rather simple by saying that flourishing comes from heeding God's laws. The so-called "second table of the law"— commandments five through ten—are a good place to start. Societies where people don't as a rule rebel against authority; where they eschew violence; don't cheat on spouses, neighbors, or the IRS; speak truthfully and use honest weights and measures; as well as give an honest day's work and are content—such a society will be blessed and will flourish. And, we should add, so will societies that honor marriage between free men and women and support the families they produce.

A second level has to do with the conditions that lead to a flourishing social order as a whole. Here, in keeping with our understanding of human dignity based on the image of God, we must affirm social and political orders where coercion is minimized and responsible moral agents are given full liberty to act and to form free associations with other human beings. Liberty is the condition sine qua non for flourishing and humane societies. Societies that shortchange liberty may achieve certain immediate goals that are attractive, but they will not flourish or last.

Let us be clear here. The description of the conditions for a flourishing society assumes something that cannot be taken for granted: This is a society *under God*. Here the wisdom of Dutch neo-Calvinism and its emphasis on *sphere sovereignty* is of great help to us. As Abraham Kuyper envisioned a flourishing society, he understood that the various "spheres"—"the family, the business, science, art and so forth"—"do not owe their existence to the state, and . . . do not derive the law of their life from the superiority of the state," but exist because of God's creative and providential power and, in the final analysis, are responsible to him alone (*Lectures on Calvinism*, 90–91). God's law, therefore, must shape the conduct of life *within* the various "spheres," and their liberty and independence *under God* are essential to human flourishing in society. To state it differently, worship of the true God, the God and Father of our Lord Jesus Christ, the Creator of heaven and earth, is the true key to human flourishing. And in a free society such as the United States of America this worship too may never be coerced; it is the task of the church to proclaim and invite people to experience such human flourishing by becoming part of the new society of Christ's own body on earth.

Discussion Questions

1. The title of this chapter is taken from Mrs. Hilary Rodham Clinton's famous book *It Takes a Village*. Without getting into a discussion (debate?) about what she intended with the title, in your experience, what do people usually have in mind when they use the phrase today? What is true and right about it? Are there potential hazards in its use?

2. Think about all the electronic innovations of the last few decades to which you have access: personal computers of all kinds, smart phones, internet, etc. Try to list all the steps of human action that needed to happen to put them into your hands. Were they all free, voluntary acts without external planning or organization, or were they at least in part involuntary, planned, and compelled?

3. Think once again about what you now have. What is essential for you to continue to be able to be a functioning participant in the digital technological revolution and all its benefits?

4. What is the shadow side of the ongoing digital technological revolution? For example, in your judgment, does the expansion of social media such as Facebook enhance community or diminish it?

5. What do you judge to be the great threats to the American experiment in ordered liberty?

For Further Reading

Bavinck, Herman. *The Christian Family.* Translated by Nelson D. Kloosterman. Grand Rapids: Christian's Library Press, 2012. Originally published in Dutch in 1908. Translation is based on the 2nd revised edition published in 1912.

Bolt, John. *"Catena sive Umbilicus:* A Christian View of Social Institutions." *Journal of Markets and Morality* 4, no. 2 (2001): 316–22. http://www. marketsandmorality.com/index.php/mandm/article/view/579/570.

———. *A Free Church, A Holy Nation: Abraham Kuyper's American Public Theology.* Grand Rapids: Eerdmans, 2001.

Eglinton, James. *Trinity and Organism: Towards a New Reading of Herman Bavinck's Organic Motif.* Edinburgh: T&T Clark, 2012.

Eliot, T. S. *The Idea of a Christian Society.* London: Faber and Faber, 1939.

Freedman, David R. "Woman, a Power Equal to a Man." *Biblical Archeology Review* 9 (1983): 56–58.

Hayek, Friedrich A. "Kinds of Order in Society." *New Individualist Review* 3, no. 2 (1964). Reprinted in *The Politicization of Society.* Edited by Kenneth S. Templeton Jr., 501–23. Indianapolis: Liberty Press, 1979. Also available online at http://oll.libertyfund.org/index.php?option=com_ staticxt&staticfile=show.php%3Ftitle=2136&layout=html#chapter_ 195376.

Klos, Jan. "Spontaneous Order versus Organized Order." *Journal of Markets and Morality* 6, no. 1 (Spring 2003): 161–76. http://www.marketsandmorality.com/index.php/mandm/article/view/494/485.

Kuyper, Abraham. *Lectures on Calvinism.* Grand Rapids: Eerdmans, 1931. Originally published as *Calvinism: Six Stone-Lectures.* Amsterdam-Pretoria, Höveker & Wormser; New York: Fleming H. Revell, 1899. These lectures were first delivered at Princeton University in 1898 under auspices of the L. P. Stone Foundation. Available online at http://www.reformationalpublishingproject.com/pdf_books/Scanned_Books_PDF/LecturesOnCalvinism.pdf.

———. "Sphere Sovereignty." Inaugural address at the founding of the Free University of Amsterdam, October 20, 1880. In *Abraham Kuyper: A Centennial Reader.* Edited by James D. Bratt, 461–90. Grand Rapids: Eerdmans, 1998.

Minogue, Kenneth R. *Alien Powers: The Pure Theory of Ideology.* 2nd ed. New Brunswick, NJ: Transaction, 2007. First published in 1985.

"Hope That Is Not Embarrassed"   4

The "Perfect" as the
Enemy of the Good

Tyranny is always better organized than freedom.
Charles Péguy

Everything begins in mysticism and ends in politics.
Charles Péguy

[A] permanent possibility of selfishness arises from the mere fact of having
a self, and not from any accidents of education or ill-treatment. And the
weakness of all Utopias is this, that they take the greatest difficulty of man
and assume it to be overcome, and then give an elaborate account of the
overcoming of the smaller ones.
G. K. Chesterton

The search for Nirvana, like the search for Utopia or the end of history or the
classless society, is ultimately a futile and dangerous one. It involves, if it does not
necessitate, the sleep of reason. There is no escape from anxiety and struggle.
Christopher Hitchens

Anyone who contemplates the tragic and sad
broken reality of our social order after the garden of
Eden will be overwhelmed by the enormity of human suffering
and pain brought about by tyranny, war, poverty, and disease. And
anyone who knows the love of God in Christ cannot be satisfied
with the way things are in this present order but will want more

and want to do more. Those who have been dramatically changed by the gospel, those who "were dead in their trespasses and sins" and "made . . . alive in Christ" (Eph. 2:1, 5), also become "a new creation" (2 Cor. 5:17) in their communities, communities that *are* different. Christians live in hope and conduct their lives in hope; that is who we are and how we ought to act.

Christian communities are different but, as we all know too well, they are not perfect and not immune from their own tragic sins, suffering, and pain. They are or should be Maranatha communities, living in eager expectation of the consummation, especially when their sins, suffering, and pain, notably under the cross of persecution, are the greatest. Yet, a strange thing has happened to many churches in the last half century, including some Reformed churches; a this-worldly transformative zeal has entered into the church as the notion has taken hold that our primary task as Christians and as churches is to change the world. Note well, this is not the same as pointing out that the Christian gospel has a transforming effect when believers fulfill their vocations in the world. Rather, this is a song about changing the world as *the* Christian calling. Reformed Christians ought to know better but, taken captive by Abraham Kuyper's famous slogan—"There is not a single square inch in the whole domain of our human existence over which Christ, who is Sovereign over all, does not cry, 'Mine!'"—they have become activists for Christ in order to transform the world.

We have become so accustomed to this rhetoric and activism that it may strike some readers as odd to raise even an eyebrow about it, much less a full-throated objection. So let me clarify. I am not suggesting for a moment that young college students, having studied abroad and seen the abject poverty of a São Paulo *favela* or the poor foraging for food in a Cairo dump, should not take on vocations that are direct responses to what they have seen: medical missions, international aid and development, and so forth. This would be a response to God's own call and we may not run away from that call as Jonah did. When God calls us, we must follow his lead.

Nonetheless, we should be concerned if the notion becomes prevalent that vocations involving intentional world transformation are the only valid callings or that all "ordinary" vocations must be intentionally transformative if they are to be legitimate. This view cannot be warranted by Scripture. The Bible simply calls us to be *obedient* to God's call and to *honor* his will in our calling through *obedient service*. Someone called to pastoral ministry, for example, is called to be faithful to the gospel and not to be a social activist. Yes, people who hear the gospel and believe it, who submit to Christ as Lord of their life, will experience change in themselves and their relationships, and thus indirectly and unselfconsciously bring about social transformation. And yes, gospel ministers are to preach the whole counsel of God, including Scriptural teaching about injustice and mammon. Furthermore, they need to call their church members to full-orbed Christian discipleship. But this must always serve the heart of the gospel, the call to sinners to repent and find in Christ forgiveness and reconciliation. One should enter the gospel ministry out of a passion to proclaim the good news that reconciles sinners to God and not from a desire to effect social or political change. That puts the cart before the horse. Concrete social changes that follow are a consequence of conversion and not the reason for conversion. To be restored into communion with God is its own good; in Jesus' opinion, the highest good. Herman Bavinck, who was no stranger to the transformative temptation, once wrote this:

> Nowadays we are out to convert the whole world, *to conquer all areas of life for Christ*. But we often neglect to ask whether we ourselves are truly converted and whether we belong to Christ in life and in death. For this is indeed what life boils down to. (*Certainty of Faith*, 94, emphasis added)

In addition to the caution about "becoming so worldly that we are unfit for heaven," there is the question of how much transformation along kingdom lines we can expect in this vale of tears. The remainder of this chapter addresses that question.

Christ's redemptive rule is not only a future hope; it is a present reality. Our Lord himself made that clear with respect to his own ministry. When he was accused by his detractors of casting out demons with the help of "Beelzebul, the prince of demons," Jesus replied by talking about a "kingdom divided against itself," and concluded with this: "But if it is by the finger of God that I cast out demons, then the kingdom of God has come upon you" (Luke 11:20; cf. 14–23). A similar self-attestation is found in Luke 7:22–23. After two of John's disciples come to Jesus and asked, "Are you the one who is to come, or shall we look for another?" (7:20), Jesus gives them this instruction: "Go and tell John what you have seen and heard: the blind receive their sight, the lame walk, lepers are cleansed, and the deaf hear, the dead are raised up, the poor have good news preached to them. And blessed is the one who is not offended by me." The actual term "kingdom of God" does not appear in this passage, but the messianic character of the claim is unmistakable as the fulfillment of the "day of the Lord" prophecies in Isaiah:

> In that day the deaf shall hear the words of a book,
>> and out of their gloom and darkness
>> the eyes of the blind shall see.
> The meek shall obtain fresh joy in the LORD;
>> and the poor among mankind shall exult in the Holy One of
>> Israel. (Isa. 29:18–19)

> Then the eyes of the blind shall be opened
>> and the ears of the deaf unstopped.
> then shall the lame man leap like a deer,
>> and the tongue of the mute sing for joy. (Isa. 35:5–6)

Returning for a moment to Jesus' ministry, here is what this new reign of God in Christ is all about: the dominion of Satan and the demons is in the process of being overthrown. The strong man is being bound (Matt. 12:29), starting with our Lord's undermining of the authority of the ruler of this world in the wilderness temptations (Matt. 4:8–11; Luke 4:5–8, 13; cf. John 12:31–32; 14:30; 16:11) and culminating on the cross where Christ "disarmed the rulers and authorities and put them to open shame, by triumphing over them in him" (Col. 2:15). The Reformed New Testament theologian Herman Ridderbos provided this summary: "All this shows that in Jesus' person and coming the kingdom has become a present reality. For the exercise of God's power over the devil and his rule has the coming of the kingdom for its foundation" (*The Coming of the Kingdom*, 63). Putting this into a helpful Augustinian contrast, E. Stauffer once said, "The all-embracing power of the *Civitas Diaboli* has been shattered, the *Civitas Dei* has broken in" (*Die Theologie des N.T.*, 105, quoted in Ridderbos, *Coming of the Kingdom*, 64).

What does this clear New Testament teaching about the present reality of the kingdom of God, or the testimony that "Jesus is Lord," mean for our passions to transform the world? First, it impresses upon us the cautionary reminder that we don't *need* to transform the world; it *has already been transformed*. If the key to the presence of the kingdom of God is victory over the prince of this world, this has been accomplished at the cross. "It is finished!" (John 19:30). Second, it points us to the nature and manner of that kingdom's effectiveness in the world as a transforming power. To put it bluntly, we need to take our Lord at his word when he told Pilate, "My kingdom is not of this world" (John 18:36).

Perhaps the most efficient way to approach this is to highlight one more passage from Isaiah that forms the text for our Lord's first sermon in his hometown of Nazareth (Luke 4:14–30):

The Spirit of the Lord God is upon me,
    because the LORD has anointed me
to bring good news to the poor;
    he has sent me to bind up the brokenhearted,
to proclaim liberty to the captives,
    and the opening of the prison to those who are bound;
to proclaim the year of the Lord's favor,
    and the day of vengeance of our God;
    to comfort all who mourn;
to grant to those who mourn in Zion—
    to give them a beautiful headdress instead of ashes,
the oil of gladness instead of mourning,
    the garment of praise instead of a faint spirit;
that they may be called oaks of righteousness,
    the planting of the Lord, that he may be glorified.
    (Isa. 61:1–3)

We face two interpretive tasks with this passage: (a) What did Jesus have in mind when he proclaimed this "good news" to his hometown? And, since Jesus' mission is uniquely his own and we must exercise great caution in applying it to our own calling as his followers, (b) what are the implications for our understanding of the kingdom of God today and our place and task in it? Does it, for example, provide warrant for Christian social activism *on behalf of the kingdom*?

The key, so it seems to me, is found in Jesus' declaration, "To-day this Scripture has been fulfilled in your hearing" (Luke 4:21). The kingdom is here! Jesus himself demonstrated the power of the kingdom through his miracles. He also gave power to the "seventy-two" whom he sent out to announce the new reign of God (Luke 10). This commission is significant in that Jesus, upon hearing the reports that "even the demons submit to us in your name," speaks about the disarming of the prince of this world: "I saw Satan fall like lightning from heaven" (Luke 10:18), imagery repeated in Revelation 9:1 and 12:9. An important point, also underscored in the Great Commission of Matthew 28:18–20, is that proclamation is the chief vehicle for "advancing the kingdom." The disciples are sent out to *announce* the kingdom and *pronounce* judgment on those who do not listen. This proclamation is authoritative; it parallels the words of ambassadors speaking on behalf of their sovereign: "The one who hears you hears me, and the one who rejects you rejects me, and the one who rejects me rejects him who sent me" (Luke 10:16).

The "today" of Jesus' Nazareth sermon is reiterated by the writer to the Hebrews (chap. 4) as a call to harken to God's voice, be renewed by the "sharper-than-any-two-edged-sword" Word of God, and enter into God's rest—i.e., the Sabbath, the kingdom of God. At the risk of belaboring the obvious, the reign of God in Christ, inaugurated in the life and ministry of Jesus, achieved in his cross and sealed in his resurrection, *is* a reality in this world, from then until now. This has been and remains the core of Christian hope, a consolation in times of suffering and loss, and an encouragement to be faithful and to obedience—"knowing that in the Lord your labor is not in vain" (1 Cor. 15:58).

This perspective is unsatisfying to those who regard it as unduly restrictive because they read Luke 4, along with other passages, as a call for direct social activism on behalf of the poor and oppressed. Christian eschatology, so it is then claimed, implies "kingdom living," and kingdom living means social and political activism on behalf of the poor, the captives, the blind, and the oppressed mentioned in the text of Jesus' sermon. We do not have the space in this chapter to examine Luke 4 (and Isaiah 61) in detail, but we ask the reader to pay attention to these verses in the light of what Jesus actually did in his ministry and what he commands his disciples to do in imitation of his ministry. The discredited attempts by liberationists to turn Jesus into some kind of social revolutionary notwithstanding, Jesus did *not* act as an agent of social, economic, or political transformation. In the words of our discussion in chapter 1, his message was *spiritual*; the good news he proclaimed was "God's favor," articulated through forgiveness. The Gospel of Mark opens with John the Baptist preaching a message of repentance that Jesus himself accents by his entry into Galilee "proclaiming the gospel of God, and saying, 'The time is fulfilled, and the kingdom of God is at hand; repent and believe in the gospel'" (Mark 1:14–15). For Jesus, forgiveness even trumps healing, as the story of the healing of the paralytic demonstrates (Luke 5:17–26).

Let's consider the dissatisfaction from another angle, the famous millennium passage in Revelation 20. At the risk of oversimplifying, the three dominant millennial views fuel different postures to this present age, human history, and culture. The premillennial view—Christ returns *before* he establishes his kingly reign on earth—tends toward a less than positive view of Christian existence as a royal calling prior to our Lord's return. In its dispensational form, it even denies the applicability of the Great Commission to the church today. The postmillennial view—Christ will return *after* believers, who live out of the victory of Christ's death and resurrection, have helped create an "extended period of righteousness and prosperity" on earth (Norman Shepherd, "Postmillennialism," in *Zondervan Pictorial Encyclopedia of the Bible*)—fuels activism, either as evangelism or social reform. The so-called amillennial view is an alternative to both, but it is mislabeled if understood to be the idea that there is no millennium. My own seminary teacher, Anthony A. Hoekema, used to say that this view was best referred to as "*now*-millennialism." Whatever the term by which this view is designated, it is a view that goes back to St. Augustine, who understood the millennium of Revelation 20 to refer to the period between the first and second coming of Christ as a time when Satan was bound "so that he might not deceive the nations any longer, until the thousand years were ended" (v. 3). The amillennial view, therefore, interprets this difficult passage in a difficult book by means of the *analogy of Scripture*, reading challenging passages in the light of the more plain and clear. In this reading, the millennium has nothing *directly* to do with peace and prosperity on earth; it is about the power of gospel proclamation to turn individuals and nations ("Go therefore and make disciples of all nations . . .") away from their enslavement, from the blind errors of their ways, to the God of heaven and earth. That's what it's all about!

I will now address the dissatisfaction I have already mentioned twice. Postmillennialists believe that a flawed eschatology like amillennialism is the reason for the church's failure to change the world. Our pessimism, they say, defeats us. In the words of Norman Shepherd, "According to postmillennialism, the major factor contributing to the observed impotence of the visible Church is the common assumption that the Gospel proclamation will not meet with success or that conditions will deteriorate before the advent. This attitude prevents the Church from laying hold sincerely upon the resources that Christ has placed at its disposal" ("Postmillennialism"). Now in fairness to Dr. Shepherd and postmillennialism, he does find the heart of Christ's kingly power in gospel proclamation. But that is not where amills like me have the problem. We are not pessimistic about the gospel's power; we fully affirm it. Nor do we deny that people changed by the gospel do change the world. We tend, rather, to look at the world with somewhat different eyes because our starting point is different.

We begin with the reality of a sinful, broken world, along with the confession that this fallen world's suffering and pain is the "normal"—though tragically abnormal—state of affairs post-Eden. As we proclaim the good news of the gospel and live obediently in the hope of Christ's present lordship and his future return, we do so with confidence that "in the Lord [our] labor is not in vain" (1 Cor. 15:58). As we look about us we see a world that gives us plenty of evidence to confirm both convictions; there is abundant evidence of original sin, but there are also many signs of transformed human existence, many places where freedom and prosperity, victory over tyranny, famine, disease, and poverty are being achieved. We therefore regard the constitutional, democratic societies of the West and their prosperity as a positive good, even a fruit of the gospel, yet not an ultimate good (that would be idolatry) but as David Van Drunen terms it, a significant *penultimate* good that should be valued and celebrated ("Importance of the Penultimate," *Journal of Markets and Morality*). This is never an uncritical celebration; the standards of a flourishing society that we sketched in the previous chapter should guide us. Where God's laws for righteous living are flaunted and where human freedom and dignity are inhibited, we voice our opposition, bear witness to the truth, and where we have opportunity advocate for change.

To borrow Thomas Sowell's term in *A Conflict of Visions*, how does this "constrained vision" of the world differ from the eschatologically driven social justice activism of today? It is helpful to consider the basis of dissatisfaction that fuels this activism. Let's return to the diagnosis and cure for what postmillennial theologian Norman Shepherd called the church's "observed impotence." The malady was diagnosed as defeatist amillennial eschatology, and postmillennial eschatology was prescribed as the cure. I am a systematic theologian who believes passionately that good doctrine is essential for the church's survival. For me, it is a question of *truth*; only the proclaimed truth of the gospel will set sinners free and equip them for obedient and holy service. *But*, I do not believe that disagreement about second-level theological reflection, such as the meaning of the millennium in Revelation 20, makes nearly as much difference as is claimed here. Of course it makes *some* difference; just not *that* much. Our daily lives of Christian discipleship are not as determined by these theological differences as some would like to think. It is hard, it seems to me, to notice major differences between two followers of Christ, both of whom live according to God's revealed law and our Lord's example of loving service but have conflicting views of the millennium. Factors other than their views on the millennium need to be taken into consideration. Doctrine is not *that* powerful. It just doesn't work that way in the Christian life—*unless*; unless the issue in fact is not the *doctrine* of the millennium but something else that becomes the standard of judgment.

I believe that this is exactly what happens, both in the case of criticism from postmillennial adherents and the social justice critique of the church's failings. The perceived problem, so it is said, is that the alleged wrong doctrine leads to the church's failure *to change the world as it should and could*. If the church were more faithful, the world would be much better than it is now. Since the world is not what it should be, there is something wrong with the church (its "observed impotence") and that must be changed. In both cases, eschatology is involved. Whereas postmills focus on the interpretation of Revelation 20, social justice activists appeal to Jesus' teaching about the kingdom of God and his ministry establishing it. In both instances, eschatological hope is used as a criterion for judging the present order of things. How should we assess this?

Let's begin with an obvious acknowledgement: Things *are* not the way they are supposed to be; not in *my life*, not in *the church*, not in *the world*. In its exposition of the second petition of the Lord's Prayer, the Heidelberg Catechism refers to all three of these (emphasis added):

> "Your kingdom come" means:
> Rule us by your Word and Spirit in such a way
>   that more and more *we submit to you*.
>
> *Preserve your church* and make it grow.
>
> Destroy the devil's work;
> *destroy every force which revolts against you*
> and every conspiracy against your Word.

> Do this until your kingdom fully comes,
> when you will be
> all in all.

We pray for the coming of the kingdom because we confess that Christ's reign will never be perfected on earth until the final consummation when the new heavens and new earth become a reality (Rev. 21–22). The most important implication of this conviction is that it leads us to resist using the perfected final consummation as *a principle of criticism* by which we challenge the present. We resist this at each of the three levels indicated in the Catechism's exposition above: the individual person, the church, and the world and human culture and society in particular. A brief comment on each.

We are sinners, saved by grace alone, and we are called to righteous, holy, victorious Christian living. This means that we are not permitted to rationalize our sins with the excuse "I am just a sinner." This would be to deny the reality of being "a new creation" (2 Cor. 5:17) and call into question the power of the Holy Spirit and the truth of the gospel. But, taking Romans 7 seriously, we also know that we are not yet able to say "we have no sin." To make that claim would be to deceive ourselves (1 John 1:8). With that in mind, we cautiously warn against Christians who speak in triumphant tones about a "Higher Christian Life" or the "Victorious Life." The great Princeton Presbyterian Benjamin Warfield, whose collected works include two large volumes on "perfectionism," provides a helpful description of the phenomenon. He observes that there are people who are impatient with the ways of God's working. "Why should the almighty Maker of the heaven and earth take millions of years to create the world? . . . Above all, in His recreation of a lost race, why should He proceed by process? Men are unwilling that either the world or they themselves should be saved by God's secular methods. They demand immediate, tangible results. They ask, Where is the promise of his coming? They ask to be themselves made glorified saints in the twinkling of an eye. God's ways are not their ways, and it is a great trial to them that God will not walk in their ways" (*Perfectionism, Part 2* in *The Works of Benjamin B. Warfield*, 8:561). The same attempt to rush ahead of the eschaton is found in the tradition of Christians who will not accept disease or poverty for Christians because they believe this is a result of failing to tap the power Christ has made available. According to health and wealth preacher Gloria Copeland, we are called to exorcize the "demon of poverty" by speaking a powerful *rhema* word against it.

In similar fashion, the history of the church is replete with protest groups who fault the churches of their day for failing to be the kind of community they romantically imagine the early church to have been. We must return, they say, to the book of Acts where all the Christians "were together and had all things in common" (Acts 2:44), and the sinful church institutions and structures that now exist were absent. Here the eschatological vision of the new heaven and new earth merges with perceptions about the ideal realization of the kingdom in the early church. And finally, the complaints about Christian failure to transform the world into the kingdom of God that result in judging all present polities and orders by the standard of the Sermon on the Mount reflect a similar lack of eschatological reserve. In each case, actual renewal change and progress are dismissed or criticized because they do not measure up to the standard of perfection the critic envisions. The "perfect" is the enemy of all earthly orders, not just tyrannies. No penultimate order can receive approval, much less praise and celebration.

I have already indicated in chapter 1 why I believe using the kingdom of God as a measuring stick for earthly realities is a serious error. I did this on the basis of biblical teaching about the kingdom of God; it is a mistake to turn the *spiritual* reign of Christ into a platform for social renewal. The biblical guidance we need comes from Old Testament law, which is itself a revealed illumination of God's creation law or norm. My point in this chapter is the converse of that case. The reality of sin is pervasive and comprehensive; Christ's victory over the devil is certain and our hope is sure. But we live between the times, and it is a mistake to let our holy impatience about the sin in our own lives, our churches, and the world lead us to triumphalist and perfectionist notions about ourselves, our churches, and the world. It is a temptation, a dangerous temptation, to fuel ambitions for the "kingdom now." Our lives as individual Christians are set up for anxiety and guilt when our "thorn in the flesh" remains; when we set the bar of sanctification or achievement at levels only appropriate to the new earth, we crush Christian spirits and often bring discredit to the gospel itself. In the church and in society it generates high levels of hostile criticism and militancy. It sets up a hierarchy where Christians of the "victorious life" sit in judgment on "mere" or "ordinary" or even "carnal" Christians. It is a form of what Luther called "a theology of glory" in contrast with a "theology of the cross." It also leads inevitably to disillusionment when the "health and wealth gospel" fails to produce the requisite BMWs and McMansions, or when all the energy poured into social justice activism fails to eliminate poverty and end war. Putting so much hope into activism that will fail in its ultimate goal is a recipe not only for disappointment but, more seriously, for embarrassing and discrediting the gospel itself.

I have tried to point in a different direction in this chapter, one that must not lead to despair or indifference. We live in hope and our eschatology must inform our understanding of Christian ethics and the way we live. The biblical vision of what is to come in the new heaven and new earth sets the brokenness of this present age into sharp relief and should fuel a holy discontent with what is. Reminding ourselves that we are pilgrims in an ethical sense, that we thus have here no abiding home, also helps us to stay detached from our possessions and be more generous toward the needy. The gospel does change people and changed people have already changed the world, not because it was their intention to build the kingdom of God on earth, but because they were compelled by gratitude to holy, obedient living. That is how the world gets changed: by gospel proclamation that gives life to dead sinners who bear witness to their renewal by their lives.

Discussion Questions

1. Do Christians expect too little from the power of the gospel to transform persons, communities, and nations? Why or why not?

2. Do you use the language of "building the kingdom" or "helping the kingdom advance" or similar phrases? What do they mean?

3. Martin Luther clearly favored a "theology of the cross" over a "theology of glory." Does the broader evangelical church in North America need to reflect upon this distinction? Does it need to think about changing its posture? What should change and what would be some of the markers that indicated changes were underway?

For Further Reading

Bavinck, Herman. *The Certainty of Faith.* Translated by Harry der Nederlanden. St. Catherines, ON: Paideia, 1980. Originally published in Dutch in 1901.

Neuhaus, Richard John. "Why Wait for the Kingdom? The Theonomist Temptation." *First Things* (May 1990): 13–21. http://www.firstthings.com/article/2007/08/002-why-wait-for-the-kingdom-the-theonomist-temptation-38.

Ridderbos, Herman. *The Coming of the Kingdom.* Translated by H. de Jongste. Edited by Raymond O. Zorn. Philadelphia: P&R, 1962.

Shepherd, Norman. "Postmillennialism." In *Zondervan Pictorial Encyclopedia of the Bible.* Vol. 5. Edited by Merrill C. Tenney, 822–23. Grand Rapids: Zondervan, 1975.

Sowell, Thomas. *A Conflict of Visions: Ideological Origins of Political Struggles.* New York: William Morrow, 1987.

Van Drunen, David. "The Importance of the Penultimate: Reformed Social Thought and the Contemporary Critiques of the Liberal Society." *Journal of Markets and Morality* 9, no. 2 (2006): 219–49. http://www. marketsandmorality.com/index.php/mandm/article/view/281/272.

Warfield, Benjamin B. *Perfectionism, Part 1* and *Perfectionism, Part 2.* In *The Works of Benjamin B. Warfield.* Vols. 7–8. New York: Oxford University Press, 1932. Reprinted: Grand Rapids: Baker, 1991.

Real-World Shalom: Markers for Human Flourishing

"To Market, to Market . . ." | 5

*Stewardship, Property,
Capital, and Morality*

If goods do not cross borders, soldiers will.
Frédéric Bastiat

As one digs deeper into the national character of the Americans, one sees
that they have sought the value of everything in this world only in the answer
to this single question: how much money will it bring in?
Alexis de Tocqueville

Civilization and profits go hand in hand.
Calvin Coolidge

Most economic fallacies derive from the neglect of this simple insight, from
the tendency to assume that there is a fixed pie, that one party can gain only
at the expense of another.
Milton Friedman

Who gets the risks? The risks are given to the consumer, the unsuspecting
consumer and the poor work force. And who gets the benefits? The benefits
are only for the corporations, for the money makers.
Cesar Chavez

It is a socialist idea that making profits is a vice; I consider the real vice is
making losses.
Winston Churchill

The author lives in Michigan, which has been hard hit by the economic realities of the new global order. During the twentieth century, Michigan was renowned for its vital industrial base, particularly the booming automobile industry. The "Big Three" made a great deal of money, as did the derivative auto parts industry, a profitability that led to generous contracts with the United Auto Workers union and a good life for auto workers. Yet, at the close of the twentieth century and during the first decade of the twenty-first century, two of the three, including General Motors, at one time the largest corporation in the world, faced bankruptcy. The reasons for this collapse all have foreign names: Toyota, Nissan, Honda, Mitsubishi, and more recently, Kia and Hyundai. Though the initial offerings of Japanese cars gave rise to the derisive and offensive manner by which North Americans identified the "Made in Japan" label with substandard goods, that changed as the twentieth century closed and the reputation for excellence followed the Rising Sun and American manufacturers scrambled to catch up. As the Asian car makers built manufacturing plants in the United States, they did not build them in Michigan but in places like San Antonio, Texas, Georgetown, Kentucky, Huntsville, Alabama, and Marysville, Ohio, not to mention Mexico. Furthermore, according to a June 2011 "Best Cars" listing in *U.S. News and World Report*, the Honda Civic (70%), the Toyota Avalon (80%), and the Toyota Sequoia (80%), all have considerably higher percentage of US and Canadian parts than do the Ford Fusion (20%), the Ford Expedition (50%), and the Buick LaCrosse (57%), not to mention the small Chevrolet Aveo (2%), discontinued after 2012 (Jim Sharifi, "How Patriotic Is Your Car?"). The automotive world has changed—dramatically!

I begin with this reality in my home state because it has generated considerable political rhetoric and moral posturing about corporate greed, obscene profits, globalization, and outsourcing and will thus serve us well in our efforts to provide a cooler, calmer, and hopefully more rational discussion of markets, "laissez-faire" capitalism, and the global economy.

Rhetoric aside, how should Christian citizens in Michigan think about all this? After the initial sense of loss and the shared pain of plant closings, unemployment, and declining communities, we need to ask, "Are these developments *morally* problematic?" When critics complain about the (im)morality of market forces that lead companies to downsize their workforce or outsource production, do they have a valid point? Do markets have a personality or power that can be judged as moral or immoral, or are markets strictly neutral? Since markets are the means by which wages, prices, and profits are determined, are critics taking a reasonable moral high road when they complain about "unfair prices" and "obscene profits" while they clamor for "fair prices" and "reasonable profits"?

The first point we need to make is that markets are "nothing"; that is to say, they are not "things." Neither in a singular form ("the market") nor in plural form ("global markets") is it proper to use market(s) as the subject of a sentence as though we are speaking of some self-standing entity with its own properties. This is often how critics of free-market economies speak of them, a tendency so prevalent that Thomas Sowell lists it as the first in order of his "myths about markets." "Perhaps the biggest myth about markets comes from the name itself. We tend to think of a market as a *thing* when in fact it is *people* engaging in economic transactions among themselves on whatever terms their mutual accommodations lead to." A market, says Sowell, "is as personal as the people in it" (*Basic Economics*, 565). Put in grammatical terms, markets are better understood as verbs than as nouns, with people as the sentence subject. Seeing the market as an entity in itself with the "power" to influence or control people's behavior is often what brings forth the critiques against "laissez-faire" capitalism. These critiques are usually accompanied by appeals for governments to regulate market activity by raising minimum wages, restricting prices (or redistributing profits), and imposing tariffs and trade barriers for the sake of fairness.

Let's consider these concerns about the morality of markets with the example of Michigan's auto industry in mind. When the Big Three were pretty much the only game in town, consumers had much less liberty of choice than they do now; their car options were limited unless they were wealthy enough to purchase, let's say, a Mercedes Benz. What changed things was competition from the Asian car manufacturers. What were the results? The immediate benefit of the competition was the vastly improved quality of all automobiles. There is no comparison between the quality, efficiency, comfort, and safety of a 1957 Chevrolet (its classic style notwithstanding) and a brand-new Chevy today. Anyone who recalls the smug dismissiveness with which North Americans derisively spoke about the initial offerings of Japanese cars in the 1960s and 1970s can't help smiling when writers for the North America auto industry now speak about how "our cars" are "catching up" to Toyota, Honda, and Nissan in quality. Market forces, i.e., customers making personal choices about buying quality cars, raised the bar for the entire industry. Free markets allow for competition and lead all actors to choices that in the end benefit others. Car companies are forced by competition to build better cars or go out of business; consumers have the choice of (perhaps) paying a little more for a quality car built by an Asian company. Why should this greater freedom and improved quality be a moral problem? Is this not, in fact, an illustration of the sound biblical principle of good stewardship?

Of course, there has been a significant human cost in the decline of the automotive industry in Michigan. This must never be discounted or overlooked. Markets do unleash destructive forces as well as new, creative ones. At the same time, however, Michigan's pain has also been a significant gain for workers and communities in those states that have added auto plants in the last decades. And since those new plants have often been added to locales that were much poorer than Michigan in its industrial heyday, is it not selfish for Michiganders to only lament about the new order of things because of its impact on our state without acknowledging the benefits to fellow American citizens? It is hard to see that this shuffling of the job deck is somehow immoral in and of itself. It too is a matter of stewardship.

Since stewardship is a high value for Christians, how do markets figure into the discussion? If a company runs the risk of bankruptcy because it has a surplus of employees and could survive by "downsizing," why should such a decision be morally problematic? Let us never try to deny or minimize the real human cost here. For people to lose their jobs and their livelihood is always a painful, traumatic event. As with all loss, people go through the stages of grief and need time to recover. Providing reasonable safety nets of protection through temporary unemployment benefits is humane and appropriate. In all such cases, however, fairness requires a consideration of the alternatives. No one benefits from a company's refusal to make difficult, painful decisions about personnel only to end up bankrupt and hurting everyone. Reasonable and fair people may disagree about whether a particular action of moving to a different locale, downsizing, or outsourcing was essential to a firm's survival, but nothing is gained by an immediate reflexive response of ranting against "obscene profits" and "corporate greed" or accusing corporations of disloyalty and failing to care about a community. Efficiency, the more stewardly use of resources that then frees them up for alternative use, is a positive biblical value and should be welcomed rather than despised. Not only are resources of wages saved made usable for improvement and expansion, we also need to think of people as resources. Losing a job does free one for a different and, perhaps, even a better one.

We need to add a separate comment or two about outsourcing and globalization. Is freer global trade only a vehicle of exploitation by which international corporations can avoid paying "decent wages" to North American workers and, by way of cheap labor in Juarez, Mexico, or Manila or China, produce cheaper consumer products for North Americans? This is the claim made by some ecumenical, ecclesiastic pronouncements such as the Accra Confession of the World Communion of Reformed Churches. Once again, we must be honest and acknowledge that environmental standards and working conditions are often substandard in many developing countries. Acknowledging the legitimate role of government in establishing appropriate environmental safeguards at home or abroad is an important consideration for Christians in business when discerning whether or not to close one plant or open another one. At the same time, it is also a little disconcerting to hear the same people who complain vociferously about the "growing gap between the rich and poor" as they compare Western standards of living with those of the developing nations to then vocally oppose relocation of North American industries to places that will lift up the economic boat for people elsewhere. A job in Malaysia or India at a wage rate that is much less than a union wage in Michigan is still a major improvement over *no job at all!* As with all economic decisions, there are trade-offs to be considered and reasonable people may disagree on them; Christians, however, should avoid demonizing those whose decisions differ from their own.

Up to this point, we have been trying to "neutralize" our understanding of market forces and choices and cool down the moral and political rhetoric that all too frequently accompanies ecclesiastical discussions and pronouncements about economics. Complaints about the "immorality" of the market and the "tyranny of profits" arise from other values that are said to be just as important as profits. We will consider more of those in the next chapter, but for now let's consider just one—loyalty. When companies close plants and move out of town, appeals are often made to certain "obligations" the corporation has to the community. And if a company moves overseas, appeals are made to "buying American" and, perhaps, boycotting corporations that are "un-American." There is much to be said for, let's say, a New England textile mill that has operated in the same community for multiple generations and served as the main provider of jobs for a community not closing and moving its operations to China where the work could be done more cheaply. But, we would be remiss if we did not also take into account the shadow side of loyalty.

Returning to our example of the automotive industry, one of the reasons that North American car companies were slow to realize the challenge posed by the Japanese auto companies was a complacent belief that customer loyalty would carry them through. Brand loyalty was a multigenerational fact prior to the growth of imports; a "Chevy family" just didn't buy Fords, and vice versa. As the Asian car manufacturers took the lessons learned from initial customer dissatisfaction and corrected the flaws in their products, they increased their market share, the Big Three market share began to plummet, and the reputations of North American car companies became tarnished. Some loyalty remained, of course; engineers who worked at Ford or General Motors took great risks should they drive an Accord or Camry onto the parking lot at work. They might be willing to sacrifice some quality for a different kind of safety. But such a choice is not entirely free; subtle and not so subtle coercion is at work. While it is not unreasonable for corporations to expect that their employees have some loyalty to their own brand, is it reasonable to expect that corporations retain interest in operations that are financially unprofitable strictly out of loyalty? In the case of corporations, what about their fiduciary obligations to their shareholders? There are always trade-offs and it is not honest to ignore them. Furthermore, when someone's deep loyalty to a particular brand—let's say to Oldsmobile or Pontiac—is killed by a corporate decision to discontinue the product, however painful the results may be, biblically it is hard to see the losses as somehow an immoral act by the corporation. The loss of "my grandfather's Oldsmobile" may seem regrettable to some, but it was not immoral.

We have been discussing the changes in the North American automotive industry in broad terms, narratively considering markets, competition, profits, and the like. We need to be more precise. Exactly how do the changes we have described come about? What are markets, really? Here is my own brief definition:

> Markets are mechanisms by which essential *information* is passed from consumer to producer, and *prices* are the vehicle by which *demand* is met by *supply*.

Markets produce the knowledge that is necessary for efficient stewardship of scarce resources. Consider the following mundane example.

Our grandchildren are coming over tomorrow and we are low on milk, so my wife asks me to pick up a few gallons on my way home from work. Let's say the price is $3.50 per gallon. How does the grocery store arrive at this price? To begin with, the price seems incredibly low when you think about it. Follow with me the journey from the cow to our breakfast table. My grandfather was a dairy farmer with a herd of about twenty-five to thirty milking cows on a self-sufficient eighty-acre farm. He and my uncle had pasture for the herd and fields dedicated to hay as well as grain (oats), and they shipped their milk to a dairy in Vancouver, British Columbia. But they needed tractors, manure spreaders, and hay balers, along with other farm equipment, and though they bred their cows to produce their own heifers for increasing the herd, they paid for artificial insemination. Then, instead of owning their own truck to bring the milk to the dairy for processing, they paid a local trucking company to do it. In other words, their ability to farm depended on the involvement of many other independent economic actors and their survival. When we get to the next step, the dairy processor has to have the equipment to separate cream, then to divide the milk up into its various cream-content levels (whole milk, 2%, skim), and also produce cheese, cottage cheese, ice cream, and so forth. Processed products have to be packaged and trucked to grocery stores where they are priced and put in dairy cases. Again, suppliers of equipment, truck drivers, and so forth, are essential, independent components of a system that gave my grandfather and uncle a livelihood and enables me to buy a gallon of milk on my way home.

For this *spontaneously ordered* system to work, each of the countless participants along the way, beginning with farm implement dealers, has to price their product or service at a level that is *just right*. If the price is too high, they will not sell their product or service. If it is too low, they will go broke. The prices cannot be set arbitrarily; they fluctuate and eventually settle (for a time!) as the information from other players in the whole process is communicated by way of prices. The one additional complication here is that government policies—subsidies and price floors for agricultural goods—also affect the price of our gallon of milk. If the Farm Bill passed by the US Congress in 2008 and scheduled to expire at the end of 2012 had not been renewed, the 1949 Agriculture Act would have gone into effect and the price of a gallon of milk potentially would have risen to $7 or $8 per gallon.

Although the individual acts of participants in the market need to be morally evaluated, asking questions about the morality of the market *as a whole* is problematic. In many respects, the market's true morality is the reality of the market itself. Markets themselves sort out the problems of what critics refer to as "price gouging" or "obscene profits" or "unfair wages." The exceptions to this are illegal activity by corporations, especially monopolistic practices, and outside interference in the market process by the state. When large corporations such as Enron provide false information to their stockholders and build huge corporate castles in "cooked books" or cyberspace, as long as the dishonesty is hidden from public view the corporation is able to make "obscene profits," obscene because they are *stolen*. But in a free-market situation, harsh economic reality intrudes and the Enrons of this world do get found out, collapse, and have their executives sent to jail. It is possible to "cook the books," but eventually the "books" have to be connected to concrete, real-world assets. *Unless* . . . unless governments step in to prevent them from the consequences of market forces that would correct their behavior. This applies not only to criminal behavior but also to "bad" corporate behavior that may not necessarily be illegal. When banks, under pressure from the government, issue subprime mortgages to people who cannot afford them and bundle them for a cascading series of resales, they engage in activity that is both bad and, finally, legally dubious. When lawmakers come to the conclusion that certain financial institutions are "too big to fail" and spend billions to rescue them from their own errors, then what is morally "obscene" is not the market but the intrusion into the market by those who have the power to manipulate the market for their own political purposes. Only the state with its coercive power to raise revenue through taxes is exempt from the market forces that correct bad and immoral economic behavior.

The previous discussion presumes a free-market context within a constitutionally ordered and protected democratic polity; in other words, the "Western" world that includes Europe and North America, along with a growing number of Pacific Rim economies. Leaving aside the complex transitional economies of nations such as China and India, we need to ask whether or not the market structures that have produced the unbelievable wealth of the West are

INTERLUDE 3

Is this chapter an apology for
libertarian, laissez-faire capitalism?

Straightforward question; easy answer: "No!" My description in this chapter is intended as a defense of free-market economies, but not as a defense of strongly libertarian, so-called laissez-faire capitalism. The latter begins with an a priori bias against all government involvement in economic transactions. That strikes me as wrongheaded from a Christian point of view. Large economic entities such as global corporations wield a great deal of power, and it is the responsibility of the state to ensure that those with much less power are treated justly. Governments must enforce laws against coercion and fraud; maintain a system that honors just measurements, weights, and currency; and govern in a manner that nurtures free association and free enterprise.

A brief word now about "capitalism." As a reluctant accommodation to general usage, in this chapter I am starting to use the word *capitalism* as a functional synonym for *free-market*. I say "reluctant" because the two terms are *not* full synonyms, and *capitalism* is both a derogatory term used by critics and a misleading term since it identifies one important ingredient of the free-market economy with the whole. "Capital" is the *fuel* of economic growth as well as its *product*. But to focus only on capital leads to the mistaken notion that the genius of a free-market order is accumulation instead of the *dynamic process* itself. My own preference is to avoid the term as much as possible and to keep the attention on the liberty of market actors and the benefits they provide to us all.

transferable to the poor, developing, and underdeveloped areas of the world. Put differently, will capitalism work elsewhere? To pose the question is itself sufficient to raise the eyebrows and evoke the protests of democratic capitalism's critics. Cries of "imperialism" ring out. Who are we to "impose" our unsustainable way of life with its materialism and consumerism on others? Once more, we need to step away from heated rhetoric and prejudice against corporations and capitalism and pay attention to the case made by someone who lives in the developing world and has amassed an abundance of information from that world to provide an answer that is cogent and based on data rather than ideology.

We turn now to the question of sustainability and the transportability of free-market economies to the underdeveloped world. The Peruvian economist Hernando de Soto and his associates at the Institute for Liberty and Democracy in Lima have done extensive studies of the actual economic activity taking place in the major urban areas of the developing world. In his book *The Mystery of Capital: Why Capitalism Triumphs in the West and Fails Everywhere Else*, here is how De Soto describes the project:

> Charitable organizations have so emphasized the miseries and helplessness of the world's poor that no one has properly documented their capacity for accumulating assets. Over the past five years, I and a hundred colleagues from six different nations have closed our books and opened our eyes—and gone out into the streets and countrysides of four continents to count how much the poorest sectors of society have saved. The quantity is enormous. But most of it is dead capital. (11)

By "dead capital" De Soto means wealth in assets that is unable to generate more wealth; assets that are "stuck" and cannot be used to do additional work but are limited to the "rigid, physical state" in which they are found. To speak in technical terms, these assets are not *fungible*. As an example, petroleum, yellow corn, and precious metals are fungible commodities; they are readily exchangeable. However, one cannot use real estate as collateral for a start-up business loan when there is no title to represent legal ownership. According to De Soto, we in the West fail to understand this reality properly because we have forgotten our own history. We simply take for granted that our assets such as real estate can be turned into capital and used for economic purposes and no longer understand the process by which this takes place. De Soto illustrates this with the metaphor of a hydroelectric dam producing electricity: "In order for capital to be creative, a *conversion* process is needed to unlock its potential. The parallel is with using the river's flowing water to produce electricity; an hydroelectric dam is the required 'convertor'" (47–48).

How then do we turn assets into a creative power for economic activity? For an answer, De Soto leans on this insight from Adam Smith: "For accumulated assets to become active capital and put additional production in motion, they must be *fixed and realized in some particular subject* 'which lasts for some time after that labour is past'" (Quoted in *Mystery of Capital*, 42). In other words, assets need to be converted to abstract concepts such as "property" or "capital" that is secured in a manner acknowledged by others and legally protected. The value of real estate, for example, depends on acknowledged ownership that can be transferred to someone else; a property without a title deed has no recognized value. Capital is not fixed by money, though money is a "standard index to measure the value of things." Property and capital are abstractions, concepts about realities such as land and houses. Proof of this fact "comes when a house changes hands; nothing physical changes. . . . Property is not the house itself but an economic concept *about* the house, embodied in a legal representation" (De Soto, *Mystery of Capital*, 50). And that is why property can be put to use.

How did this order of laws about property and titles come into being? A history lesson is important here because there was no overall purpose or intentionality that created it, no global design; the initial intention was simply "the mundane purpose of protecting property ownership." Since it is impossible "for assets to be used productively if they do not belong to something or someone," we need to "confirm the existence of these assets" and establish our ownership and right to use them by a "formal property system" (permanent records and registries, titles, legal rules about transfer, and so forth) (46). De Soto retraces for us how property becomes capital within such a system, which allows the value of property to become an exchangeable asset: "Formal property records and titles thus represent our *shared concept* of what is economically meaningful about any asset. They capture and organize all the relevant information required to conceptualize the potential value of an asset and so allow us to control it. Property is the realm where we identify and explore assets, combine them, and link them to other assets. The formal property system is capital's hydroelectric plant. This is the place where capital is born" (47, emphasis added).

As De Soto points out, "While houses in advanced nations are acting as shelters or workplaces, their representations are leading a parallel life, carrying out a variety of addition functions to secure the interests of other parties." In sum: "Legal property thus gave the West the tools to produce surplus value over and above its physical assets" (51). The international capitalist market order was not designed; it arose spontaneously from the use of property rights that themselves were not initially intended to become the engines of economic progress. In confirmation of De Soto's thesis, the crucial role of private property rights as the key to prosperity and civilization is defended in far greater historical detail in Tom Bethell's *The Noblest Triumph: Property and Prosperity through the Ages*. Furthermore, "property" or "capital" is not simply a synonym for a nest egg, for "money saved and invested." Proof of this is the fact that "Third World and former communist nations" inflate their economies with money "while not being able to generate much capital" (De Soto, *Mystery of Capital*, 44).

Let us now return to the question whether free-market economies—or capitalism, if you will—is transferable beyond the

INTERLUDE 4

Isn't God against "private property"?

Christian critics of democratic capitalism frequently take issue with the notion of "private property." After all, it is said, God is the only true "owner" of everything and we are only his stewards. We don't "own" any property; we are only commanded to use it wisely. This is very pious and true but can be applied in two quite different ways. For pious progressives, because, in their judgment, many people do not use what they own for the "common good," appealing to God's ownership helps ground an argument in favor of curtailing the accumulation of personal property and redistributing it. The state then serves as God's instrument for the common good by redistributing property. The difficulty with this understanding is that the responsibility for being God's steward is taken away from individuals and transferred to a small group who presumably know best what is good for all. Alternatively, within the bounds of law, appealing to God as the absolute owner also serves to undergird the responsibility given to free and moral people to be stewards of the property God has entrusted to them. In this view, there is a strong presumption against state confiscation of property to redistribute to those deemed needy. The second view seems like the natural implication from the Sabbath and Jubilee legislation of the Old Testament that restored ancestral land inheritances so families could again have the opportunity to be stewards.

world of the Western democracies. According to De Soto, we need to take a closer look at what has already happened. The story that emerges from his investigation is eye opening and the figures strain credulity. De Soto points out that after 1950, "there began in the Third World an economic revolution similar to the social and economic disruptions in Europe in 1800." Machinery was introduced that reduced the demand for rural labor, and new medicines and public health initiatives helped cut infant mortality and extend life spans. As a result, people flocked to the cities. "In

China alone, more than 100 million people have moved from the countryside to the cities since 1979" (17). These new urban poor have created an enormous amount of wealth in assets such as real estate, but it is "dead capital" because "the institutions that give life to capital—that allow one to secure the interests of third parties with work and assets—do not exist" there (16). What staggers the mind is the total value of this dead capital as it was estimated by De Soto and his associates, estimates that he judges to be "as accurate as they can be and quite conservative":

> By our calculations, the total value of the real estate held but not legally owned by the poor of the Third World and former communist nations is at least $9.3 trillion. (35; see table 2.1 on p. 36)

To make this very concrete, consider what De Soto says about Haiti. "In Haiti, untitled rural and urban real estate holdings are together worth some $5.2 billion. To put that sum into context, it is four times the total of all the assets of all the legally operating companies in Haiti, nine times the value of all assets owned by the government, and 158 times the value of all foreign direct investment in Haiti's recorded history to 1995" (33).

This is a tragic reality that cries out to heaven. As we consider the plight of the Haitian poor and think of their hard work that remains so unrewarded, our sense of justice is profoundly disturbed. Perhaps because it is so close to us and we know it so well, Haiti is the perfect case for our consideration of what will work to improve their lives. Haiti's reality and that of places in the world that resemble that nation easily overwhelm us; so much needs to change—attitudes, habits, cultures, laws, governments, and the list goes on. Stopgap solutions calling for Third World debt forgiveness or some other form of redistribution become attractive until we realize that not only do they not fix structural barriers to prosperity but also completely fail to honor the dignity of the poor themselves as creative and productive image bearers of God. Remember, there is this unbelievable abundance of assets that cannot be utilized for growth and prosperity! De Soto's book both discourages us with its sad tale and encourages us by reminding us that things are not hopeless. After all, the developed legal order that secured property rights in the West took several centuries to unfold; it did not happen overnight. Today, we stand at the other end of that history and knowing what we do about what is required to lift the poor out of their misery, we should not feel hopeless. With informed assistance from those of us who are well-to-do and powerful, we can hope that it does not take the poor in Haiti as long to emerge into a more prosperous future.

We have not come close to exhausting the subject of markets and morality. In particular, we have not paid attention to any possible shadow side of our freedom to choose and to consume. That is the subject of the next chapter.

Discussion Questions

1. Does the word *capitalism* connote something negative or positive for you? What do you understand by the term?

2. Is "capitalism" Christian? Is "capitalism" contrary to Christian convictions and practices? If so, which ones?

3. How does Hernando de Soto's analysis of poverty in the Third World strike you? Is it too simplistic? If so, what factors does he overlook?

4. Anticipating the material of the next chapter, what are the common Christian complaints about free-market capitalism?

For Further Reading

Bethell, Tom. *The Noblest Triumph: Property and Prosperity through the Ages.* New York: St. Martin's Press, 1998.

Blank, Rebecca M., and William McGurn. *Is the Market Moral? A Dialogue on Religion, Economics, and Justice.* Washington, DC: Brookings Institution Press, 2004.

De Soto, Hernando. *The Mystery of Capital: Why Capitalism Triumphs in the West and Fails Everywhere Else.* New York: Basic Books, 2000.

Norberg, Johan. *In Defense of Global Capitalism.* Washington, DC: Cato Institute, 2003.

Sharifi, Jim. "How Patriotic Is Your Car?" *U.S. News and World Report,* June 30, 2011. http://usnews.rankingsandreviews.com/cars-trucks/how_american_is_your_car/.

Sirico, Robert. *Defending the Free Market: The Moral Case for a Free Economy.* Washington, DC: Regnery, 2012.

Sowell, Thomas. *Basic Economics: A Common Sense Guide to the Economy.* 4th ed. New York: Basic Books, 2011. First published in 2000.

Free to Be (Ir)Responsible?

*Liberty, Consumerism,
and the Problem of Walmart*

The forces in a capitalist society, if left unchecked, tend to make the rich richer and the poor poorer.
Jawaharlal Nehru

Capital as such is not evil; it is its wrong use that is evil. Capital in some form or other will always be needed.
Mohandas Gandhi

Advocates of capitalism are very apt to appeal to the sacred principles of liberty, which are embodied in one maxim: The fortunate must not be restrained in the exercise of tyranny over the unfortunate.
Bertrand Russell

Modern capitalism needs men who cooperate smoothly and in large numbers; who want to consume more and more; and whose tastes are standardized and can be easily influenced and anticipated. . . . What is the outcome? Modern man is alienated from himself, from his fellow men, and from nature.
Erich Fromm

The inherent vice of capitalism is the unequal sharing of blessings; the inherent virtue of socialism is the equal sharing of miseries.
Winston Churchill

[G]overnment's view of the economy could be summed up in a few short phrases: If it moves, tax it. If it keeps moving, regulate it. And if it stops moving, subsidize it.
Ronald Reagan

In the previous chapter we presented the case for free-market capitalism—within the framework of a legal order that secures property rights—as the engine for economic growth and the hope for the world's poor. The benefits of such a free and competitive market order, sometimes termed "neoliberal," are nicely summarized by Christian economist Rebecca M. Blank: (1) "it provides *incentives for productivity*," (2) it "fosters *efficiency*," and (3) it "requires *no central direction or organization*" ("Viewing the Market through the Lens of Faith," in Rebecca M. Blank and William McGurn, *Is the Market Moral?* 15–16). Furthermore, a free and competitive market works remarkably well in reducing poverty. Earlier this year an issue of the international journal *The Economist* called attention to the astonishing fact that from 1990 to 2010 "nearly 1 billion people have been taken out of extreme poverty" ("Towards the End of Poverty," June 1, 2013). As a result, United Nations officials are resetting the Millennium Development Goals they drew up in 2000 (which expire in 2015) because the goal of halving global poverty in fifteen years has been met in ten, the article reported. How did this widely unreported development happen? "Most of the credit . . . must go to capitalism and free trade, for they enable economies to grow—and it was growth, principally, that has eased destitution." And again, "the biggest poverty-reduction measure of all is liberalising markets to let poor people get richer." With this insight also comes a warning. To those "[m]any Westerners [who] have reacted to recession by seeking to constrain markets and roll globalisation back in their own countries, and . . . want to export these ideas to the developing world, too"—don't! "It does not need such advice. It is doing quite nicely, largely thanks to the same economic principles that helped the developed world grow rich and could pull the poorest of the poor out of destitution" (Ibid.).

All this is unquestionably true; empirical historical comparisons with other economic orders—feudal, mercantilist, or centrally planned—show that societies with ordered liberty generate untold wealth and raise living standards for all their citizens.

However, should this entail a wholehearted or enthusiastic endorsement of free-market capitalism by Christians? The late Irving Kristol in *Two Cheers for Capitalism* captured what I judge to be the right posture. Kristol explains the positive but muted title of his book this way:

> A capitalist society does not want more than two cheers for itself. Indeed it regards the impulse to give three cheers for any social, economic, or political system as expressing a dangerous—because misplaced—enthusiasm. (ix)

This sense of free-market polity as a *penultimate* good comports well with the eschatological reserve discussed in chapter 4. In fact, this is its great virtue; we are not encouraged to judge it by some utopian standard. As we take a look at the limitations of a free-market order in this chapter, we recognize that many of its critics do just that. Kristol notes that this "habit, so ingrained in the modern political imagination . . . is quite pernicious," even "explosive" and "self-destructive," and contrasts it with the modest and restrained realism of the vision undergirding free-market capitalism:

> A capitalist order, in contrast [with the utopian vision], begins with the assumption that the world is full of other people, moved by their own interests and their own passions, and that the best we can reasonably hope for is a society of civil concord, not a community of mutual love. (ix–x)

In other words, we ought to judge our economic order by the *economic benefits* it brings us and not by the final eschatological hope of the kingdom of God. Nor should we expect our economies to bring us the kingdom of God on earth. In Kristol's words, "a capitalist order has a keen sense of its own limitations"; it does not point to higher, more noble values or transcendent truths and ideals. "It does not celebrate extraordinary heroism in combat, extraordinary sanctity in one's religious life, extraordinary talent in the arts," and so forth. At the same time, "it does not necessarily denigrate such things either, but, in contrast to previous societies organized around an axis of aristocratic or religious values, it relegates them to the area of personal concern, whether of the isolated individual or of voluntary associations of individuals. Only there may we find 'love, the beloved republic'" (x). In other words, do not expect our economies to save us and don't unduly criticize them for their failure to be our saviors. They can't and shouldn't be expected to save us. This does not mean carte blanche approval of all that takes place in our economic order either, only that its failure to bring the kingdom of God on earth should not be part of our critique.

In what follows in this chapter I do want to explore several of the key criticisms leveled against the democratic capitalist order, but I want to place them within a context. When it comes to our economic life as North American Christians, we can go in several directions. Since we benefit greatly from the economic order in which we live, we can be grateful and accept it as a providential blessing. At the same time, we are also keenly aware that our own position of privilege is not universally shared. There are far too many people in our world, including some on our continent, who live in varying levels of poverty. This fact leads others to become critics of our economic system and to plead for another one. Gratitude and critique are both appropriate in proper proportion and proper relation to each other. Christians err when they are grateful for what they themselves enjoy if this is accompanied by indifference to those who do not share the blessing. Similarly, prophetic zeal about the world's poor that fails to acknowledge the gifts and blessings of freedom and prosperity that accompany our economic and political order is no less an error. In considering key criticisms or challenges to the order of democratic capitalism, we want to keep the preceding cautions in mind. We want to acknowledge the blessings of our political and economic order without lapsing into self-satisfaction by ignoring the plight of those who live outside of its bounty. And we want to listen to and take seriously the key critiques of that order without forgetting to be grateful for what it has accomplished and what it continues to produce. So, to take a phrase from Rebecca Blank, let's take an honest look at the market "through the lens of faith."

Blank's own assessment is balanced and wonderfully wise as she answers the dilemma in her own tough question: "If we accept an economic model that assumes appropriate choices are made when individuals are self-interested, individualistic, and focused on the acquisition of more things, is doing so a validation of our worst natures and a turning away from Christian attributes?" ("Viewing the Market through the Lens of Faith," 22). This is an overwhelming list of human vices that ought to trouble Christians. Is it a deal breaker for Christian endorsement of free-market capitalism? In what follows I will discuss some of the concerns Blank addresses (though in my own way), bring up additional issues, and follow this with a brief reflection on the importance of and the risks involved in human freedom.

Issue 1: Religious and moral neutrality— Does the market push us all toward nihilism?

The market, I have said, is a neutral process of free and moral people making individual choices. By itself, the market is neutral about those choices; it has no preference for "good" choices over "bad" choices, however defined. The market passes no judgment on an heir who, like the prodigal son, blows his inheritance on wine, women, and song instead of developing a responsible and productive life plan and supporting kingdom causes. Conversely, the market is not a tyrant demanding that all human associations be reduced to market forces of supply and demand requiring cost-benefit calculation. It's not difficult to recognize the distortion that takes place when marriages, families, friendships, or the church are treated as market realities instead of the spiritual and moral realities they are. Of course, turning the Christian faith into a "consumer product" and running churches as though they were competing for greater "market shares" is *not* a consequence of our participation in a market economy as such but brought about by church leaders mistakenly importing market ideas into an area of life where they do not belong.

This last example, however, does point to a real challenge for Christians living in our democratic, capitalist, socio-economic-political order. The market is ubiquitous and rather overwhelming and, in good measure, its very neutrality strikes us as a moral problem. For starters, Reformed Christians are especially wary of designating something as "neutral." Abraham Kuyper's famous line about Christ owning every "square inch" does not fit well with the notion of leaving alone such a huge arena of human activity as the economy and calling it "neutral." To clarify, I am not suggesting that specific actions by participants in the market—entrepreneurs, inventors, and consumers—are beyond religious concern or morality. All participants in the market should be governed by a moral compass with a view to serving a moral purpose. Consider here a parallel with eating. There are moral rights and wrongs with respect to food; there is sin (gluttony) and there is worship ("whether you eat or drink . . . do all to the glory of God," 1 Cor. 10:31). These higher (or lower!) purposes, however, are not intrinsic to the acts of eating and drinking as such. They arise out of our religious-spiritual-moral nature as God's image bearers. Am I making too much of this distinction? Some might even suggest that I am, in fact, in error when I keep speaking of the market as a basically neutral reality and warning against expecting anything eschatological from it. No, they say, we need to see our economies restructured in such a way that they more and more reflect the values of the kingdom of God where, for example, there are no poor.

Admittedly, there does seem to be something of a case against the market's neutral *amorality*. While it does not *force* choices on us, the market does seem to *encourage* individualism, hedonism, and the acquisition of more and more "stuff," as the validation of the "good life." The healthy functioning of a market system— as the foundation of a prosperous society—does seem to require sustained and continuous *economic activity* by its members. Don't we all benefit when an economy grows and hurt when there are downturns? Perhaps, one could argue that, in some sense, spending, buying, and consuming are even a civic duty. This is the whole theory behind so-called Keynesian economics, inspired by British economist John Maynard Keynes (1883–1946), which holds that times of unemployment and economic recession are caused by a lack of "aggregate demand" (the sum total of a society's demands) and can be reversed by government fiscal and monetary policy that puts more money in the hands of consumers. When people have more money, they buy more, leading producers to make more, and supposedly everyone is happy. Doesn't this mean that the principle "more is better" is built right in to market economies? That could be a problem for a Christian moral framework. Without getting into an academic argument about Keynesian economics, including the critiques of economists such as Friedrich Hayek (1899–1992), Ludwig von Mises (1881–1973), and Milton Friedman (1912–2006), let us tackle the issues of neutrality and growth, addressing the latter by considering two important problems with the "more is better" philosophy: *consumerism* on the individual level and *sustainability* on the larger or macro level.

It is important to highlight the sense in which we are speaking of the market as "neutral." We are not speaking of the *actors* in the market, only of market *structures* and *processes* such as property rights, free exchange and trade, capital formation and investment, the right to form corporations and trade unions, and so forth. These are neutral in the same way that eating and drinking are neutral as formal activities, though *what* one eats and *how* or *why* one eats of course is not. In the same way, *what* market actors do as well as *why* and *how* they do it remains religiously and morally significant even when the market itself is neutral. In free

---

INTERLUDE 5

Don't "neutral" markets call for a Christian alternative?

Neutral markets, we have already noted, do not mean neutral participants. A free market provides all the permission we need to fulfill our calling to be disciples of Christ. This does not satisfy some who want our economic order itself to be more reflective of kingdom values. But, what would an alternative "Christian economic order" look like? Would markets not be free? What then happens to liberty? In fact, longings for a more "Christian" economic alternative, one more in keeping with the kingdom of God, often expressed in terms of a "third way" beyond Left and Right, beyond individualist capitalism and collectivist socialism, are frequently little more than ill-disguised attempts to pose as alternatives to themselves. Upon closer inspection, they turn out to be similar or even identical to the—generally leftist—binary left/right alternative. Although *Sojourners* magazine, founded and edited by Jim Wallis, once billed itself as a "progressive Christian voice with an alternative vision for church and society, beyond both the religious right and the secular left," the actual policy prescriptions of its "biblical alternative" viewpoint are practically indistinguishable from its secular counterpart. It is hard to imagine an order that honors liberty and provides opportunity more than the one we presently enjoy.

markets, Christians are free to acknowledge that Jesus is Lord; in fact free societies enable and enhance the flourishing of Christian discipleship.

The economic growth that is so integral to our order does, nonetheless, place Christians before a conundrum of sorts. In affirming the liberty that is essential to it, we open the door to the materialist temptation reflected in a consumerist mentality, and we run into the question of sustainability—can we keep up this engine of growth without sating and dulling our souls and running out of planetary resources?

Let's begin with the phenomenon of *consumerism*, which is perfectly captured by the bumper sticker slogan "Born to Shop." Seriously, is it possible for people to be *that* superficial? Apparently, yes. One need not possess the highest level of spiritual discernment to recognize the foolishness of consumption for the sake of consumption. The problem of acquisitiveness, of wanting more and more beyond the levels of necessity, however, is not restricted to societies with flourishing market economies. The biblically mentioned sins of Achan (Josh. 7), King Ahab (1 Kings 21), Elisha's servant Gehazi (2 Kings 5:19–27), Judas (John 12:4–6), and Ananias and Sapphira (Acts 5) all happened long before Adam Smith and the celebration of free-market economies. Acquisitiveness is not an institutional flaw but a personal human failing. And, above all else, it is a religious-spiritual-moral failing for which the antidote is the gospel truth that "one's life does not consist in the abundance of his possessions" (Luke 12:15), along with our Lord's warnings against the idolatry of mammon (Luke 16:13; cf. 1 Tim. 6:10). The church's proper response to the sin of consumerism is not to denounce the market but to expose the sins of the human heart and offer the gospel as liberation.

The base sin here is *materialism*, the belief that our lives will be happier and more fulfilled when we have more stuff. And since even our legitimate desires—food, drink, shelter, and companionship—are insatiable, enough is never enough. Without pleading for including "shopaholism" as a genuine mental disease to be catalogued in the *DSM-5* (*Diagnostic and Statistical Manual of Mental Disorders*), we do note that acquisitiveness is addictive. As with all addictions, we need more and more to get the same satisfaction, a satisfaction that becomes ever more elusive because, as Christians know, idols only destroy. This cycle can continue until a person is reborn by the Spirit of God and experiences the "rest" of soul that can only be found in God. Augustine was not the first to experience such rest, but he expressed it so well: "[Y]ou have made us for yourself, and our heart is restless until it rests in you."

This antidote applies to *personal* and *individual* consumerism. Our stuff does not define us. But that is not the whole story. Even at the personal and individual level, in our thinking we need to go beyond the immediate and obvious act of walking into a shopping mall or outlet store with a bundle of cash in our pocket and throwing our cash at one thing after another. That crude form of shopping is increasingly rare; we now do it with plastic cards and transfers made by electronic signals; our wealth now resides in virtual bank vaults of numbers in cyberspace. Once again, though the "system" does not force us into acquiring debt, it does seem to encourage it since swiping a debit or credit card is so effortless and painless. We don't even feel like we are spending real money. This "consumer debt," and the materialism on which it is based, also applies to societies as a whole. It is not only individuals that overspend and go into deep debt; nations do it as well. The spiritual disease at the heart of materialism is the passion to live only for the present moment, to gratify immediate desires, to acquire more and more without any thought for tomorrow.

It is here that we encounter the market economy as one of the prime symbols of the modernist challenge that is directed at the very heart of the Christian faith. When sociologist Peter Berger wanted to capture the pressures of the modern worldview in a single phrase, he spoke of "the heretical imperative." The word *heresy* comes from the Greek word *hairesis*, which means "choice," and Berger's point was that modernity's signal accomplishment was the multiplication of consumer choices. From the dozen or more different toothpastes or deodorants available in our drugstores to churches competing for our participation to whether or not to have children, or even whether or not to let a pregnancy go to full term, choices dominate our lives as modern people. At this point we can appeal to the freedom we have as individuals to make choices that comport with God's revealed will for our lives and say no to the tyrannies of modern choice—and we would be right. We can choose simplicity and refuse to participate in the excesses of market idolatry. We *can* just say no!

Yes, we can, but just like Mrs. Nancy Reagan's far too breezy "just say no to drugs" slogan of the 1980s, this underestimates the powerful, even religious draw of modernity's siren song. Few have captured the nihilistic tenor of the modern ethos as succinctly and elegantly as theologian David Bentley Hart has in his book *Atheist Delusions: The Christian Revolution and Its Fashionable Enemies*:

> [W]e live in an age whose chief value has been determined, by overwhelming consensus, to be the inviolable liberty of personal volition, the right to decide for ourselves what we shall believe, want, need, own, or serve. The will, we habitually assume, is sovereign to the degree that it is obedient to nothing else and is free to the degree that it is truly spontaneous and constrained by nothing greater than itself. (21–22)

It is at this deeper and more profound level that we need to confront the sin of consumerism:

> We [moderns] are, first and foremost, heroic and insatiable consumers, and we must not allow the specters of transcendent law or personal guilt to render us indecisive. For

us, it is choice itself, and not what we choose, that is the first good . . . ."[C]hoice". . . often seem[s] to exercise an almost mystical supremacy over all other concerns. (22)

Fatalistic resignation is not the appropriate response here. The potential personal and social pathologies of market idolatry are no reason to repudiate free-market economies altogether; they are calls to look more closely at the spiritual and moral foundations of the culture that is needed to make it flourish. That is the point of Michael Novak's groundbreaking work *The Spirit of Democratic Capitalism*. Novak sees a flourishing market economy as one of "three dynamic and converging systems functioning as one: a democratic polity, an economy based on markets and incentives, and a moral-cultural system which is pluralistic and, in the largest sense, liberal" (14). As Pope John Paul II observed in his encyclical *Centesimus Annus* ("On the Hundredth Year"), the problem of consumerism cannot be resolved from within the market itself (*CA*, § 36, condensed version repr. in Richard John Neuhaus, *Doing Well and Doing Good*, 297). Nor, we must add, can the passing of laws by the state cure it; as a spiritual-moral problem this has to be addressed from within the moral-cultural sphere by churches rather than legislatures. In the words of John Paul II, "To overcome today's individualistic mentality we require *a concrete commitment to solidarity and charity*, beginning with the family" (*CA*, § 49; repr. in Neuhaus, *Doing Well and Doing Good*, 301). Resistance to the market's pull toward acquisitive consumerism requires spiritual resources; providing them is what the church is singularly called and equipped to do as she bears witness to the gospel. Instead of simply denouncing the market as many contemporary church pronouncements do, we need to concentrate on cultivating and nurturing the spiritual disciplines that equip us to resist the siren songs of advertisers to buy and spend, spend and buy. Economic growth and increasing prosperity are not identical with consumerism; though it is a demanding challenge—recall our Lord's observation about camels and needles—one can be both wealthy and a faithful steward of God's gifts.

The spiritual disciplines that are required to be faithful in this area of our life are important in their own right. The real spiritual problem with trying to fix market pathologies by coercive laws that curtail freedom is that this is a legalistic strategy that also inhibits moral and spiritual growth. Laws on their own change no hearts.

Issue 2: Sustainability—Can we keep this up?

Do we really want to resist the market altogether? Is economic growth really a *moral* problem? Don't we need growth? According to Michael Novak, not only does "the natural logic of capitalism lead to democracy," it provides prosperity for the poor through economic growth. "Democratic polities depend upon the reality of economic growth" (*Spirit of Democratic Capitalism*, 15). Why should we resist the market's pull to produce and consume more and more when it even serves a greater good? How could we be opposed to helping the poor?

We need to distinguish growth that takes place within appropriate boundaries of responsible stewardship from unrestricted and unbounded growth for growth's sake. The human imaginative capacity for making junk and peddling rubbish is unbounded, and Christians need to be discerning participants in the vast and wonderful global market. This is true for both entrepreneurs and consumers. Both need to ask: "Just because we can, should we?" The consumer question is not just "Can we afford it?" but "Is it a 'good purchase'?" As adults we need to apply to ourselves the parental advice we should be giving to our children: "Yes, we can afford it, but good stewardship means saying no to this purchase." I will repeat here the admonishing words of Dorothy Sayers in her essay "Why Work?" cited earlier in chapter 2: "We should ask of an enterprise, not 'will it pay?' but 'is it good?'; of a man, not 'what does he make?' but 'what is his work worth?'; of goods, not 'can we induce people to buy them?' but 'are they useful things well made?'; of employment, not 'how much a week?' but 'will it exercise my faculties to the utmost?'" (132–33). Work, after all, "is not, primarily, a thing one does to live, but the thing one lives to do" (134–35).

At the same time, we need to ask whether there are "limits" to growth because of limited resources, as the title of a famous 1972 book commissioned by the Club of Rome proposed. Put differently, is economic growth an unqualified good? The question places us before a real moral dilemma. On the one hand it is clear that only economic growth will lift the earth's poor out of their misery. Wealth does not fall from the trees; it is produced by human effort and grows when work is productive and profitable. Our heart for the poor must lead our heads to be positive about growth. At the same time, we are mindful of the spiritual dangers of a "more is better" mentality; we have already considered the depth of our spiritual illness as modern people who bow at the altar of choice and acquisitiveness. The dilemma is nicely captured by John Paul II in his encyclical: "It is not wrong to want to live better; what is wrong is a style of life presumed to be better when directed towards 'having' rather than 'being'" (CA, § 36 repr. in Neuhaus, *Doing Well and Doing Good*, 297). There is also a second dimension that we must now consider.

The drive to produce and consume more and more is not only a spiritual-moral problem corroding the soul, it is also an ecological challenge. Can planet Earth sustain a level of resource utilization and consumption in which everyone in the world lives like we do? Are its resources not finite, and does the Christian commitment to stewardship of God's world not therefore challenge any

Christian endorsement of free-market capitalism? Undoubtedly it was concerns such as this that led Ronald Sider to endorse the proposal by the authors of *Limits to Growth* that we voluntarily choose to live by a standard so in the end "everyone can share the good earth's bounty" without destroying the environment or harming God's creation (*Rich Christians in an Age of Hunger*, 269; cf. 149–59, 187–90).

Addressing the constellation of issues behind such a proposal is not easy. While it would appear to be a commonsense conclusion that the world's resources are somehow fixed and that when we run out of something it is gone, never to return, the matter is not nearly so simple as that. Paul Ehrlich's 1968 neo-Malthusian tract, *The Population Bomb*, became the Bible of the environmental movement and its alarmist, apocalyptic message led a movement for Zero Population Growth along with draconian proposals to curb the human birth rate. The book opens with this statement: "*The battle to feed all of humanity is over. In the 1970s hundreds of millions of people will starve to death in spite of any crash programs embarked upon now. At this late date nothing can prevent a substantial increase in the world death rate.*" In a 1971 speech, Ehrlich predicted that "by the year 2000 the United Kingdom will be simply a small group of impoverished islands, inhabited by some 70 million hungry people . . . If I were a gambler, I would take even money that England will not exist in the year 2000." Another Ehrlich prediction on Earth Day 1970 involved sea life: "In ten years all important animal life in the sea will be extinct. Large areas of coastline will have to be evacuated because of the stench of dead fish" (quoted in Ronald Bailey, "Cracked Crystal Ball: Environmental Catastrophe Edition," *Reason*, December 30, 2010). When challenged about the accuracy of his predictions *after* they had obviously been proved wrong, Ehrlich responded in a manner worthy of the Millerites, Jehovah's Witnesses, and others whose specific predictions about the return of Christ failed to come true—he changed the timing. "It's already started, you just don't see all of it yet, and it is still going to happen in a big way later, just not now." Largely in response to Ehrlich's book and its dire predictions, in 1980 economist Julian Simon placed a scientific wager before him about the scarcity and price of natural resources. Simon asked Ehrlich to pick five commodity metals— Ehrlich picked chromium, copper, nickel, tin, and tungsten—and bet that their price would decrease by 1990, while Ehrlich bet that they would increase. Between 1980 and 1990, the world's population grew by more than 800 million, the largest increase in one decade in all of history up to that point. Nonetheless, the price of each of the five metals *decreased*. Ehrlich's $1,000 investment ($200 per commodity) in 1980 was worth $423.93 in 1990. Simon won the bet ("Simon-Ehrlich wager," *Wikipedia*).

Perhaps the doomsayers are wrong; perhaps the world's resources *can* sustain the kind of growth needed to lift up the poor more permanently; perhaps the world's standard of living across the board *can* be significantly raised. At the very least, it would be the worst form of cruelty not to even consider the possibility that Julian Simon was right in his repudiation of the Ehrlich scenario that has been publicly repeated so often that it is now conventional wisdom among the elites of our day:

> It also is sure by now that these beliefs are entirely wrong. Though it is not well-known to the public, there is broad scientific consensus that the air and water in the United States are getting cleaner rather than dirtier, that natural resources are becoming less scarce rather than more scarce, and that there is no quantitative evidence that population growth is detrimental to economic growth in poor countries or rich ones. (Julian Simon, *Hoodwinking the Nation*, 1)

My point in inserting Paul Ehrlich and his failed prophecies into the discussion here is not to provoke an academic debate about how to measure the finiteness of the world's resources. Nor is it to suggest that Christians can be sanguinely indifferent to responsible stewardship of the world's resources. Instead, I want to ask what is missing from the doomsday scenarios leading the Paul Ehrlichs of this world to make such colossal misjudgments. Two things are absent, so it seems to me. The first is a failure to account for the biblical teaching about God's providence. Christians who live in hope need to be wary of doomsday apocalyptic scenarios. In the second place, Ehrlich-like prophecies fail to take into consideration the world's number one resource: human ingenuity, creativity, imagination, and industriousness. It is startling, for example, to read in the 1991 Club of Rome report, *The First Global Revolution*, that because divided nations require a common enemy to unite them now that communism is dead, the new enemy would be humanity itself.

> In searching for a new enemy to unite us, we came up with the idea that pollution, the threat of global warming, water shortages, famine and the like would fit the bill. In their totality and their interactions these phenomena do constitute a common threat which must be confronted by everyone together. But in designating these dangers as the enemy, we fall into the trap, which we have already warned readers about, namely mistaking symptoms for causes. All these dangers are caused by *human* intervention in natural processes, and it is only through changed attitudes and behavior that they can be overcome. The real enemy then is humanity itself. (Alexander King and Bertrand Schneider, *The First Global Revolution: A Report by the Council of the Club of Rome*, 70, 75)

This is an astonishing statement that intentionally ignores the vast improvement of human life and longevity along with the improvement in quality of our natural environment in the free countries of the world. Nuclear power and natural gas are far more environmentally friendly than coal or wood as sources for our heat. Automobiles have done their worst in cities like Los Angeles, but the crucial work of horses in nineteenth-century New York or London did not leave those cities cleaner than they are today. Modern technology, modern medicine, and modern transportation and communication all utilizing computer chips (who would have thought that sand, i.e., silicon, could become so lucrative!) have made life better for all except those who are prevented from participating in the modern, global economy. The point is that before the invention of the internal combustion engine the black gold under the Arabian sand was worthless. *Human* ingenuity, creativity, inventiveness, and entrepreneurial zeal are the engines that have improved the human condition. And the Club of Rome thinks that we are the *enemy*! The misanthropic cruelty of this thesis is overwhelming, especially as we think about what it means for leaving the world's poorest poor in their misery. The divide could not be greater; those whom the Club of Rome calls the "enemy," ostensibly for the sake of saving the planet (not to mention enhancing the power and wealth of certain elites!), Christians, in solidarity with all fellow image bearers of God, celebrate as the "solution." That is the perfect segue to our consideration of the third moral allegation often made against the market economy.

Issue 3: Loving our neighbor— Does self-interest make us selfish?

This section will be brief because our discussion of discontent about market economies will continue into the next chapter where we devote its entirety to the issue of greed and envy. Let's begin by clarifying the important difference between self-interest and selfishness. In a *New York Times* article titled "Can Businesses Do Well and Good?" (January 6, 2009), Harvard economist Edward L.

Glaeser declared, "Adam Smith made the case for *selfishness* when he wrote that 'it is not from the benevolence of the butcher, the brewer, or the baker, that we expect our dinner, but from their regard to their own self-interest'" (Quoted in David Larson, "Adam Smith: Selfishness or Self-Interest," *Spectrum*, January 23, 2009, emphasis added). It is disappointing that a Harvard economist fails to read Smith carefully and correctly despite the fact, as David Larson notes, that "Smith explicitly and constantly distinguished the concepts, condemning the first [selfishness] and condoning the second [self-interest]" (Ibid.). Smith was simply *describing* what he observed in terms of what he believed people *knew*, and not speculating about the deeper *motives* of their hearts. And he most definitely was *not prescribing* the moral posture of selfishness. Many critics of his use of "self-interest" and the "invisible hand" fail to acknowledge that Smith's great work on economics, *The Wealth of Nations* (1776), was preceded by his publication of *The Theory of Moral Sentiments* (1759). Morality, he argued in that earlier work, does not proceed from reason but from sentiment or feeling, particularly the feeling of sympathy. We become moral when we imaginatively are able to enter into and empathize with the feelings of others. What the two works have in common is the suspicion with which Smith regarded the reign of autonomous reason. *Ordinary* people normally understand their own interests better than philosophers or politicians. With respect to morality, he rejects reason in favor of feeling. With respect to economics, Smith rejects the notion that a superior *reasoning* mind could direct the economic order to a desirable outcome. In Larson's words Smith's point is that "because they are *self-interested*, the butcher, brewer, and baker look out for themselves; however, because they are *not selfish*, they also care for their customers" ("Adam Smith: Selfishness or Self-Interest"). According to Smith, this means, among other things, that "the poor man must neither defraud nor steal from the rich," even though the benefit to the starving poor man is far greater than the loss would be harmful to the rich man (*Theory of Moral Sentiments*, vol. 1, pt. 3, chap. 3). Smith is not a utilitarian!

Scripture teaches clearly that we must love our neighbor. This is a nonnegotiable rock of moral principle for Christians. Knowing how to put that into practice requires spiritual discernment and the wisdom of prudence. Even someone committed to the free market and the legitimacy of self-interest cannot but notice and be troubled by the dislocations it brings about. Thanks to its corporate purchasing power, Walmart has been an enormous blessing for consumers. The poorer among us can purchase things they desire at affordable prices. This is a good thing! Nonetheless, when Walmart puts up one of its large stores at the edge of a town, it often does lead to smaller shops and stores going out of business. Understandably, moral as well as aesthetic sensibilities are offended, especially when a large corporation like Walmart treats its suppliers ruthlessly. One "big-box store" puts "Main Street" out of business and a town's character and charm are irremediably altered. Free markets do create losers as well as winners.

Can anything be done about these dislocations, or are they simply the price that must be paid for "progress"? Economists like to refer to this process of change in the market as "creative destruction," first labeled as such by Austrian economist Joseph Schumpeter (1883–1950). It is necessary for some industries to change or even die if we want economic progress. Famous examples include the demise of horse-drawn carriages—leading to the unemployment of buggy-whip manufactures, farriers, and coachmen, among others—and the move toward diesel and electric locomotives, putting firemen and stokers on the unemployment line. In our day we could decry the digital revolution for its elimination or reduction of telephone operators, store checkout clerks and bank tellers (thanks to scanners and ATMs), and even postal carriers. At the same time—to continue with our illustration from

INTERLUDE 6

Are you saying we will be saved
through technical progress?

No! Of course not! Only Jesus saves. The category is inappropriate here because there is no economic "salvation" short of the consummation. Nor should we make an idol of technical progress as though we are to passively accept injustice or abject poverty while waiting for a technical fix. We need to utter strong warnings against unrealistic and utopian hopes placed in technology as savior. My only point in the preceding was to encourage an end to knee-jerk responses to the creative-destructive forces of the marketplace by recognizing the potential for greater good in them as well. We must carefully weigh our response to the effects of market dislocations and traumas and balance short-term benefits with long-term consequences, acknowledging that there are always prudential trade-offs to be made. And we do this knowing that our well-intentioned efforts to do good for people by trying to save their jobs always have unintended and unknown consequences. Saving good jobs for a few today may lead to many more of us becoming paupers tomorrow.

the previous chapter—Henry Ford's innovations brought thousands of Southern poor to Michigan in the first half of the twentieth century to work on Big Three assembly lines, creating new jobs for poor people that lifted them into the middle class, not to mention providing transportation for the masses. We could multiply examples of this sort in transportation, communication, agriculture, manufacturing, and retailing, as we shall discuss in the next chapter. The point is that loss of one kind of work does not mean loss of all work, period. In fact, the loss of some jobs and their substitute or replacement by machinery or technology should be regarded as a good. The earthmoving machines built by Caterpillar, for example, liberated men from a great deal of backbreaking, body-destroying physical labor. Something may be lost; usually, much more is gained. Nevertheless, Christians in business in these circumstances should not lose their moral compass; cutthroat ruthlessness in trying to beat out competition and ignoring all human costs is not an appropriate corporate strategy for someone who follows Christ.

Without in any way minimizing the cost to people brought about by the market's creative destruction, we must not only keep our eyes focused on the longer-term benefits, we must also ask ourselves about alternatives. Would it be better to provide for a more orderly, regulated way of making these transitions? Is it even possible? We need to say a few words about the calls that come forth for more government regulation to prevent corporations from making profit-based decisions that will hurt people. How do we respond when someone says, "There ought to be a law!"?

In conclusion, I believe that it is important today to underscore the theme of liberty. We should start with the premise of liberty and then carefully—*very carefully*—consider policies that would ameliorate the worst consequences of the changes and dislocations that are bound to happen. Theologically speaking, liberty is foundational because that is also how God created us and how he deals with us. According to Herman Bavinck, God tolerates sin and evil because he "is able to govern it in an absolute holy and sovereign manner." We were not created as puppets and social policy should not treat people as mere "stocks and blocks" of voters. "If God had not allowed [sin and evil] to exist, there would always have been a rationale for the idea that he was not in all his attributes superior to a power whose possibility was inherent in creation itself. For all rational creatures as creatures, as finite, limited, changeable beings, have the possibility of apostatizing." Nonetheless, God did not forestall the possibility of human rebellion and sin. "But God, because he is God, never feared the way of freedom, the reality of sin, the eruption of wickedness, or the power of

INTERLUDE 7

Don't we need **some** *external*
regulation of the market?

The ideal of absolute libertarian freedom, of complete *laissez-faire* capitalism, is a fantasy, whether it is celebrated by followers of Russian-American novelist Ayn Rand or pilloried by critics. Markets only work well in the framework of law that helps create a free culture of honesty and trust. So, of course there must be regulation that reflects concerns about worker safety and health, environmental responsibility, honest bookkeeping, integrity of contracts, truth in advertising, safety of quality products, and the like. But, since this is a point on which supporters and foes of capitalism alike tend to agree, it is not where critics focus their attention. The call for more regulation often seeks to block the forces of creative destruction in order to shield people from experiencing its pain. This then takes the form of passing a law that so penalizes corporations that it becomes too expensive for them to innovate, relocate, or outsource. These regulations might help buffer the immediate hurts of creative destruction, but the cure is worse than the disease. Inefficiencies and new market realities are then ignored; the important information companies need to make necessary changes is distorted; and, finally, while a company's demise might be slowed down, especially if it is subsidized by the state, its end is sure. The laws of economics are a demanding and cruel master and cannot be flaunted forever; payment is required and will be made. We have ample evidence from attempts to regulate economies in a global fashion for the benefit of the "people" (such as the planned economies of socialism and communism) that they don't work and lead to tyranny. In the end, as Dostoyevsky's Grand Inquisitor (in *The Brothers Karamazov*) knew so well, we do have to choose between the ideal of liberty or the promise of security. Of course, neither is absolute; the challenging task for policy makers and citizens is to strike the just balance between them.

Satan." Bavinck then goes on to quote Augustine: "Because he knew he was absolutely able to control sin, 'he deemed it better to bring good out of evil than not to permit any evil to exist at all" (*Reformed Dogmatics*, 3:64–65).

"God, because he is God, never feared the way of freedom. . . ." As children of God, set free in Christ, we can do no less. Whenever we are tempted to set aside human liberty for the sake of greater security, we need to pause and consider God's own ways. We will not overcome evil by coercion; our weapons are the spiritual ones of persuasion, truth telling, and obedience. Neither freedom nor security is an absolute; God made us free and promises that he himself is our real security. This is also what we proclaim to the world: "For freedom Christ has set us free; stand firm therefore, and do not submit again to a yoke of slavery" (Gal. 5:1). Of course the apostle Paul had in mind here the external observance of Jewish law and not the modern polity of democracy and free markets. My point here is not to use a biblical text to defend the latter, but to impress upon the reader that the spiritual freedom we have in Christ did change the course of human history as Christian believers refused to bow the knee to earthly sovereigns because only Jesus was Lord. In the course of human events, it was this conviction that to be human is to be free rather than a slave to another human being, however exalted, which led to orders of economic polity that honored human freedom and dignity. And, furthermore, since it is part of our "normal" (sinful) nature to resist freedom and responsibility for the sake of greater security, whether that be in religious moralism and legalism or in polities where freedom is curtailed, we need to affirm liberty with boldness. In sum, the message the church needs to proclaim to the world today is this: "We are free! Put your security in the God who made heaven and earth, upholds the cosmos, and governs history. Build no Towers of Babel! Do not bow the knee to Babylon!"

At the end of this chapter, the reader might wonder how this all fits together. We should favor the free market in free societies, a conviction that leads to growth and prosperity. At the same time we need to rein in our own materialist impulses to acquire more and more. And then, though we need to be wary about imposing limits on growth, we also need to be responsible stewards. Don't some of these ideals clash with each other? Isn't this rather messy? Isn't it even risky? What if we do run out?

Indeed it is complex and messy. One of my goals in this chapter was to make that very point and to discourage the notion that there are neat and tidy ways to eliminate the messiness and, above all, to warn against draconian attempts to curtail human freedom and development in the name of neatness, whether it be called "fairness" or "equality" or "sustainability." We lack the knowledge to create such a world; we have no choice but to live with the mess. But isn't that the very nature of the human condition? We live in faith, faith in God's providential rule over all things, including our material well-being. Our order was made possible because of faith in Providence and that is a fitting segue to our next chapter.

Discussion Questions

1. Are you ever embarrassed by your wealth? Why or why not? Should you be?

2. Do you try to shop local even if you could save money on Amazon or other internet providers? Do you go to big-box stores instead of local suppliers?

3. Should we as Christians be willing to pay more for goods and services that buck the trend of corporate growth in order to keep smaller operations in business or provide "fair trade" for people overseas? How much would you be willing to pay? Are there limits? Can you think of unintended consequences?

4. Put yourself in the place of a member in a small town's council. Your council has before it a request for a permit from Walmart (or some other big-box store) to build on the outskirts of town near the highway. There has been a great deal of pressure from

your fellow townspeople to say no! Several of the town's merchants and tradespeople are members of your church, and saying yes potentially puts them out of business. Discuss the factors that you as a Christian must take into consideration as you come to a decision.

5. When you are able to afford something, how do you decide whether or not it is a "good purchase"?

For Further Reading

Abela, Andrew V. "The Price of Freedom: Consumerism and Liberty in Secular Research and Catholic Teaching." *Journal of Markets and Morality* 10, no. 1 (Spring 2007): 7–25. http://www.marketsandmorality. com/index.php/mandm/article/view/260/251.

Bailey, Ronald. "Cracked Crystal Ball: Environmental Catastrophe Edition." *Reason*, December 30, 2010. http://reason.com/blog/2010/12/30/ cracked-crystal-ball-environme.

Bavinck, Herman. *Reformed Dogmatics*. Vol. 3, *Sin and Salvation in Christ*, translated by John Vriend, edited by John Bolt. Grand Rapids: Baker, 2006.

Berger, Peter. *The Heretical Imperative: Contemporary Possibilities of Religious Affirmation*. Garden City, NY: Anchor Press, 1979.

Bethell, Tom. *The Noblest Triumph: Property and Prosperity through the Ages*. New York: St. Martin's Press, 1998.

Black, Robert A. "What Did Adam Smith Say about Self-Love?" *Journal of Markets and Morality* 9, no. 1 (Spring 2006): 7–34. http://www. marketsandmorality.com/index.php/mandm/article/view/310/299.

Blank, Rebecca M. "Viewing the Market through the Lens of Faith." In Rebecca M. Blank and William McGurn. *Is the Market Moral? A Dialogue on Religion, Economics, and Justice*, 11–56. Washington, DC: Brookings Institution Press, 2004.

Hart, David Bentley. *Atheist Delusions: The Christian Revolution and Its Fashionable Enemies*. New Haven and London: Yale University Press, 2009.

King, Alexander, and Bertrand Schneider. *The First Global Revolution: A Report by the Council of the Club of Rome.* New York: Pantheon Books, 1991. http://ia700408.us.archive.org/31/items/TheFirstGlobalRevolution/ TheFirstGlobalRevolution.pdf.

Kristol, Irving. *Two Cheers for Capitalism.* New York: Basic Books, 1978.

Larson, David. "Adam Smith: Selfishness or Self-Interest." *Spectrum,* January 23, 2009. http://spectrummagazine.org/node/1368.

Meadows, Donella H., Dennis L. Meadows, Jørgen Randers, and William W. Behrens III. *Limits to Growth: A Report for the Club of Rome's Project on the Predicament of Mankind.* New York: Universe Books, 1972. An abbreviated version is available online at http://www.bibliotecapleyades.net/sociopolitica/esp_sociopol_clubrome6.htm. Updates were published in 1992 and 2002, and a forecast for the next forty years was published in 2012.

Neuhaus, Richard John. *Doing Well and Doing Good: The Challenge to the Christian Capitalist.* New York: Doubleday, 1992. This book is an extended meditation on John Paul II's 1991 encyclical *Centesimus Annus* (cited as *CA* in this chapter), which is included in this work, in condensed form, as an appendix, pages 285–304. Citations of this encyclical are to the condensed Doubleday version.

Novak, Michael. *The Spirit of Democratic Capitalism.* New York: American Enterprise Institute / Simon & Schuster, 1982.

Schlossberg, Herbert. *Idols for Destruction.* Nashville: Thomas Nelson, 1983.

Simon, Julian. *Hoodwinking the Nation.* New Brunswick, NJ: Transaction, 1999.

Wikipedia contributors. "Simon-Ehrlich wager." *Wikipedia, The Free Encyclopedia.* http://en.wikipedia.org/wiki/Simon-Ehrlich_wager. Accessed May 15, 2013.

"Towards the End of Poverty." *The Economist,* June 1, 2013. http://www.economist.com/news/leaders/21578665-nearly-1-billion-people-have-been-taken-out-extreme-poverty-20-years-world-should-aim.

"It Isn't Fair!"

Providence, Privilege, Gratitude,
Guilt, and Equality

Thou shalt not covet . . . anything . . .
Exodus 20:17; Deuteronomy 5:21

I have learned in whatever situation I am to be content. . . . In any and
every circumstance, I have learned the secret of facing plenty and hunger,
abundance and need.
The apostle Paul, Philippians 4:11–12

For the love of money is a root of all kinds of evil.
The apostle Paul, 1 Timothy 6:10

He who is not contented with what he has, would not be contented with what
he would like to have.
Socrates

Envy: Feeling bitter when others have it better.
Rebecca Konyndyk De Young

Dad: The world isn't fair, Calvin.
Calvin: I know, but why isn't it ever unfair in my favor?
Bill Watterson

Few can fail to be moved by the contrast between the luxury enjoyed by some
and the grinding poverty suffered by others.
Milton Friedman

$\mathbb{E}$arlier we made the point in chapter 5 that, properly speaking, the market is not a "thing" in its own right; it is better to think of the market process as a verb than as the subject of a sentence. Perceptive readers may have wondered if we mildly transgressed against our own maxim in the previous chapter when we acknowledged that market forces often seem to have a life of their own; they appear as "actors" when the consequences of market processes hurt people and we feel powerless to avoid them or control them. The destructive-creative power of market forces may be productive and beneficial in the long run, but they still hurt people in the short run. Yet, even then, we need to distinguish the moral behavior of the participants from the market's essentially neutral process. We must maintain the distinction or resign ourselves to becoming the market's slaves. Spiritual resistance to the idolatry of mammon, difficult enough under the best of circumstances, as our Lord observed in his comments about "camels" and "needles" (Matt. 19:24), understandably becomes an even greater challenge in a growth-oriented, materially successful culture. Challenging, yes, but not impossible, lest we deny the power of the Holy Spirit and the grace of sanctification.

In the previous chapter we noted Michael Novak's description of democratic capitalism as a complex tripartite order of dynamic, converging systems: a democratic polity, a market economy, and a moral-cultural sphere committed to liberty. Our concern here is with that "third rail" of democratic capitalism, the spiritual, moral, cultural realm. Novak follows other observers of the American experiment in ordered liberty, such as Alexis de Tocqueville, in emphasizing the crucial importance of the moral-cultural realm for maintaining the other two. "Theologically speaking, the free market and the liberal polity follow from liberty of conscience" (Novak, *Spirit of Democratic Capitalism*, 112). Putting this into more operational terms, human flourishing of a free people in a free-market economy requires a morally strong, virtuous people. And it's just at that point that we encounter the first of the market's alleged "sins" that are the focus of this chapter.

Accusation 1: The market is self-destructive.

In *The Cultural Contradictions of Capitalism*, a classic analysis of democratic capitalist societies, Daniel Bell, then professor of social sciences at Harvard University, argued that capitalism harbors within itself the seeds of its own destruction. By creating a desire among successful people for personal gratification and accumulation, it corrodes the virtues required to make it work successfully in the first place, namely, a strong work ethic, delayed gratification, frugality, and so forth—all the so-called "bourgeois" or middle-class values. In addition, it also creates a leisure class that tends toward the transgressive "avant-garde." The avant-garde sees itself, in the words of French revolutionary thinker Henri de Saint-Simon (1760–1825), as a "priesthood" with the responsibility to help society march into a glorious future: "This is the duty of artists, this, their mission" (quoted in Bell, *Cultural Contradictions of Capitalism*, 35). In other words, the taboo-breaking artist is the revolutionary harbinger of a liberated glorious new age. When we consider the vulgarity of our contemporary popular culture, a culture that transgresses all boundaries because it refuses to recognize any, it seems clear that the avant-garde has become the commonplace. We lack the moral virtues and cultural habits required for a democratic polity with a free economy, and we have put in their place a hedonistic, self-absorbed way of life that is increasingly a global reality. Can we survive it?

We may find an answer to that question in an unlikely place: Christian medieval monasticism. Monasticism arose in the early church *in part* as a reaction to Christianity's own success. "In part" needs to be emphasized here because many, like the famous early

ECONOMIC SHALOM | JOHN BOLT

monk Antony of Egypt (AD 251–356), simply heard the words of Jesus to the rich young ruler to "go, sell what you possess and give to the poor" (Matt. 19:21) as a personal call. Nonetheless, even then, the fact that Antony came from an affluent family, and that many other young men from similar circumstances joined him, does indicate that Christians were no longer a persecuted, marginalized, and poor minority in the Roman Empire. The imperial acceptance of Christianity with the Edict of Milan in AD 313 simply acknowledged that Christians had "arrived." For our purposes, however, it is the monastic reform movements of the ninth through eleventh centuries AD that interest us.

There is a proverbial observation, found in other religions as well as in Christianity, that "monasteries tend to get rich and monks fat." From the sixth century AD to the present, Christian monasticism in the West has followed the Rule of Saint Benedict (ca. AD 480–547). However, the disciplined life and hard work by monks yielded great wealth for the monasteries, which, in turn, led to a loss of discipline and willingness on the monks' part to do hard work. Reforms at specific abbeys, such as the Cluny Abbey in 910, were initially effective, but the reform monasteries themselves succumbed to the same cycle, leading in turn to additional reforms such as those at Cîteaux Abbey in 1098. The Cistercian reforms also lacked permanence and eventually gave rise to the Trappist order at La Trappe Abbey in 1664. To complete the picture, we also need to mention the rise of the mendicant orders in the thirteenth century, the Franciscans and the Dominicans, which were founded on the ideal that monks need only their begging bowls. The exemplary ideal of Saint Francis notwithstanding, neither order was able to maintain its ideological devotion to poverty.

This brief history of monasticism underscores the necessity of distinguishing the *process* and *activity* of the market, not to mention its *results*, from the *capacity* of its participants for free, responsible, moral action. We are not forced to become materialists; we are not slaves to the market. The task of spiritual resistance to the idolatry of mammon is difficult and demanding, and the failure to retain the victories won in early monastic reforms is discouraging. But, looking at the glass as half-full instead of half-empty should encourage us; the Holy Spirit does move godly Christians in concert to desire renewal and to work at their own sanctification and the sanctification of their communities. In the history of the church, there is never good reason for adopting a counsel of despair; that remains true today in *our* challenging times.

With this in mind, let us now consider the most important omission in our discussion of the previous chapter, namely, a serious consideration of *sin*. We can think of countless sins that can and do take place in the market, such as dishonesty, theft, shoddy workmanship, waste of natural resources, laziness, greed, monopolies and cartels, the corrupting influence of advertising to create new consumer "needs," profiteering—the list goes on. However, the striking thing about this list is that most of these sins are not restricted to a free-market economy but apply equally well to any society—Old Testament Israel, a feudal or mercantilist order, or a socialist or communist system. They are part and parcel of the broad range of human sins and follies. We therefore conclude that while the moral-cultural base of liberal polities and free economies may be eroding in the Western world, the human participants— who are free to sin as well as to act justly—are still moral agents who can repent, turn from sinful ways and habits, and in turn bring healing and renewal to their cultures and societies. Blaming the economic order for the sins and follies of its participants misplaces the responsibility and averts us from any possible remedy. We are not victims fated to a prospect of cultural and social decline. That brings us to the second charge against free-market economies.

Accusation 2: Free markets generate monopolies that undo market forces.

The logic of this charge seems impeccable. Thanks to the purchasing power acquired by economies of scale, giant retailers such as Walmart, Home Depot, and Best Buy expand by driving out smaller retailers. Eventually, one would think, the "big boys" just take over, create monopolies, and destroy the market itself. This seems logical, but history tells a quite different tale. Consider only three retail giants of the twentieth century: A&P; Montgomery Ward—the Walmart before Walmart—and Kmart.

From the 1920s through the 1960s, A&P (The Great Atlantic & Pacific Tea Company) was the leading grocery chain in the United States. Thanks to innovations, volume buying, and vertical integration, A&P squeezed out smaller neighborhood grocers, greengrocers, butchers, bakers, and dairymen. In a review of *The Great A&P and the Struggle for Small Business in America* by Marc Levinson, Jay Weiser notes that "as late as 1939, A&P had more supermarkets with sales over $250,000 than all other American retailers combined" ("The Big Store: The Mythology of Small Business Meets a Retailing Giant," *The Weekly Standard*, April 29, 2013, 34). Observing the trajectory of A&P conquests in the first half of the twentieth century, one could reasonably conclude that by the turn of the next century A&P would be the only grocery retail chain left standing. Today, however, the brand has disappeared. Changing social realities such as suburbanization and improved home refrigeration, along with confiscatory state chain-store taxes and federal government regulatory assaults such as the Robinson-Patman Act of 1936, all combined with the rise of other supermarket chains, such as Safeway, not only slowed down the A&P juggernaut, but eliminated it altogether.

The story of Montgomery Ward is similar. Started in the nineteenth century as a mail-order retailer, it used high-volume purchasing and efficient delivery from its enormous warehouse in Chicago to become the world's largest retailer by the turn of the century, when a competitor was created by Richard Sears. Both Montgomery Ward and Sears, Roebuck, & Company, however, were out to lunch when it came to seeing the opportunities for actual department *stores* in America's growing urban centers, a failure seized upon by another visionary entrepreneur, James Cash Penny. To make a long story short, Montgomery Ward's path to becoming a retail giant monopoly was not only derailed but stopped short by 2001, when the last Ward's department store closed. Sears and J.C. Penny remain, but they continue to have their struggles.

The story of Kmart begins with Sebastian S. Kresge opening a five-and-dime store in downtown Detroit in 1899. By keeping prices really, really low, Kresge stores survived the Depression and competition from Sears, Ward, and J.C. Penny, eventually leading to the larger Kmart discount department stores in 1962. Notwithstanding aggressive marketing strategies and innovative merchandising agreements (e.g., with Martha Stewart Living), Kmart filed for Chapter 11 bankruptcy protection in 2002 and merged with Sears, Roebuck & Company in 2004 to make the Sears Holdings Corporation the third largest US retailer, though they were listed thirteenth in the annual *STORES* magazine Top 100 Retailers report (July 2013). Yet according to Yahoo Finance's online Industry Center, "Kmart remains the #3 discount retailer in the US, behind Walmart and Target," but big does not necessarily make better. A 24/7 Wall St. article titled "Eight Retailers That Will Close the Most Stores" reported that Sears will close 100 to 125 stores in 2013 and Kmart another 175 to 225. Closing anywhere from 13 to 16 percent of one's stores (out of 2,118 total) does not look like a recipe for creating a monopoly.

These three tales from the arena of retailing could be multiplied in the spheres of newspapers and news magazines, transportation, utilities, and the communications industry (telephone, radio, television, internet), among others. We do not have the space to consider all the factors that not only prevented large retailers from becoming monopolies but even caused them to decline and, in some cases, to disappear. My only point in entering these brief accounts is to urge caution against a rush to judgment about economic realities that we see before us right now and that lead us to call for regulatory measures that would prevent developments we judge to be alarming. When we begin to see patterns of success and failure (e.g., downsizing and outsourcing), we inevitably hear the outcry "There ought to be a law against this!" Not so fast! While we must indeed be on the lookout for genuine monopolies and cartels (they are rare), we must also remember that the market itself is self-correcting. "The key to a monopoly," as a judge of the 9th Circuit Court of Appeals once pointed out, "is not market share—even when it is 100 percent—but the ability to keep others out" (Sowell, *Basic Economics*, 179). The rise and fall of retail giants proves that markets and open competition work, and that is to say nothing yet about the enormous benefits to consumers from retailers such as Walmart.

Accusation 3: The market is the cause of poverty and misery in the world.

Our third charge is the most serious and sustained and requires the lengthiest response. Critics of the political and economic order we have been affirming usually try to make their case by pointing to the great chasm between us in the West and the world's poor. The blame is then placed on the rich for creating the poor; they are poor *because* we are rich. The Accra Confession of the World Communion of Reformed Churches mentioned earlier, for example, takes its point of departure in the reality of "a scandalous world that denies God's call to life for all." "The root causes of massive threats to life," it proclaims, "are above all the product of an unjust economic system defended and protected by political and military might." The evidence for this is the disparity between rich and poor, reflected in the fact that "the richest 1 per cent" have an annual income "equal to that of the poorest 57 per cent." The crisis of this disparity is caused by "the development of neoliberal economic globalization," which "makes the false promise that it can save the world through the creation of wealth and prosperity, claiming sovereignty over life and demanding total allegiance which amounts to idolatry." In response, the Accra Confession calls for Reformed Christians to "acknowledge the complicity and guilt of those who consciously or unconsciously benefit from the current neoliberal economic global system" and "confess our sin in misusing creation and failing to play our role as stewards and companions of nature."

We could multiply such claims from affluent individuals and churches in the West who, in the name of biblical prophecy, denounce the very structures that have given them their prosperity. It is important for us to note that the blame for the wretched condition of the world's poor is laid directly at the feet of what is derisively called "the current neoliberal economic global system." Professor Nicholas Wolterstorff alleges the same thing in his book *Until Justice and Peace Embrace*. Denying that poverty and misery are the default condition of fallen humanity, he also dismisses the claim that "the underdeveloped nations just need more free enterprise" as mere self-interest on the part of its advocates. Wolterstorff then provides his own explanation for Third World poverty:

> In the first place, the mass poverty of the Third World is for the most part not some sort of natural condition that exists independently of us; quite the contrary, a good deal of it is the result of the interaction of the core of the world-system with the periphery over the course of centuries. In

many areas there has been a development of underdevelopment, and we in the core have played a crucial role in that development. (86)

We do not have the space here to enter into a full debate about "world-systems theory" or its kissing cousin, "dependency theory" ("core" versus "periphery"), except to say that there is a strong historical argument against the notion that markets make the rich richer and the poor poorer. The facts do not appear to be on Wolterstorff's side. As Michael Novak has noted, "[u]nder market economies, the historical record shows unprecedented gains in real incomes for the poor." Novak then points to the extensive research by British economist Lord Peter Bauer, which shows that "the nations least touched by market economies are poorest, and within nations those regions least open to markets are in the worst economic and human shape" (*Spirit of Democratic Capitalism*, 109). We would add to this the recent report in *The Economist*, noted at the beginning of the previous chapter, that "nearly 1 billion people have been taken out of extreme poverty" in the decade from 1990 to 2000, and that "[m]ost of the credit . . . must go to capitalism and free trade, for they enable economies to grow—and it was growth, principally, that has eased destitution" ("Towards the End of Poverty," June 1, 2013).

Rather than getting bogged down in a statistical skirmish, my question is, what is the alternative being proposed to liberal polity and free markets? And here the critics become infuriatingly vague and rain down on us guilt-ridden platitudes instead of clear alternatives. Here is a list of the things that the Accra Confession rejects:

- ✧ "the current world economic order imposed by global neoliberal capitalism"

- ✧ "the unregulated accumulation of wealth and limitless growth"

- ❖ "any ideology or economic regime that puts profits before people, does not care for all creation and privatizes those gifts of God meant for all"
- ❖ "any theology which affirms that human interests dominate nature"

Positively, the Accra Confession asks for certain commitments:

- ❖ "to seek a global covenant for justice in the economy and the earth in the household of God"
- ❖ "to work with other communions, the ecumenical community, the community of other faiths, civil movements and people's movements for a just economy and the integrity of creation"

Cruelly, it does not tell us how to achieve these wonderful goals.

Similarly, Professor Wolterstorff speaks eloquently and poetically about "justice in shalom" in chapter 4 of *Until Justice and Peace Embrace* but acknowledges that he has not "suggested alternative practices and alternative institutional arrangements and regulations." He then becomes coy: "And where we do not have examples of alternative practices . . . we have plenty of suggestions. Our contemporary academics have not been lax in producing suggestions for how things might be handled differently." The real problem, he suggests, is that we *know* what needs to be done but are unwilling; we are all slaves of our own self-interest (142–43). The poor remain poor because we are selfish.

My response will be more theological and pastoral than academic and economic. We know all too well the awful reality of poverty, malnutrition, and suffering in our world. When we, who are well-educated, comfortably housed, well-fed, and with superb medical care, become aware of the slums of Calcutta, the *favelas* of

Brazil, and the shantytowns of South Africa and see the faces of the malnourished children of Eritrea and the Sudan on our evening news, our Christian consciences instinctively cry out and we feel deep down in our hearts that this just isn't fair. And this is as it should be; at a deep emotional level, we *know—this is not the way it's supposed to be!* But how do we frame our response? How do we "explain" it, and what should we do about it?

Enormous disparities of wealth are troubling to everyone; they troubled Adam Smith as well as the late Chicago economist Milton Friedman, famous for his defense of the free market. In his book *Free to Choose*, Friedman spoke of "gross inequities of income and wealth" which "offend most of us" and declared: "Few can fail to be moved by the contrast between the luxury enjoyed by some and the grinding poverty suffered by others" (146). But, though it offends our spiritual and moral sensibilities, is it "unfair," or, more properly, is it *unjust*? Is the phenomenon of inequality prima facie proof of injustice that must be remedied by the application of social justice?

"It isn't fair that . . . !" Every parent has heard the complaint—more than once, or even twice. Whether it is a brother getting a bigger piece of pie or a younger sister getting a later curfew, the occasions for making comparisons and complaining in the intimate setting of a family are almost infinite. Wise and skillful parents will find ways of acknowledging that "indeed, life *is* unfair" without "provoking to wrath" (Eph. 6:4; Col. 3:21) or giving further opportunity for more envy. Do children make the complaint simply because they have a native sense of justice and a keen sense of its violation? Or, does it come from a more shadowy side of their hearts? The answer, most likely, is that it is a little of both. Children do have a good sense of justice and an eye for injustice. At the same time, the cry "it isn't fair" also gives evidence of the capital sin of envy. If Mom gives you a generous piece of blueberry pie for dessert, is it really a big deal that your brother's piece is a smidgeon bigger?

The same thing is true on a larger social level. Imagine the following *fictional* situation: I am a social worker in a Christian adoption agency; my wife and I live in a modest home and own only one vehicle—a fifteen-year-old minivan—for which we have to negotiate a schedule. Our children receive a good Christian education, are even able to take music lessons, and we go camping—in a tent!—for our summer vacations. My cousin, on the other hand, coming from exactly the same socioeconomic circumstances as me and attending the same schools, became a highly successful entrepreneur, who in addition to his palatial home in the city owns a "cottage" on Lake Michigan that is twice the size of our house. He owns three vehicles, including a crossover SUV with a ski rack, all manufactured by the Bavarian Motor Works, and in the winter takes his family vacationing to Vail, Colorado. Is this disparity a moral problem? If I obsess about the disparity and lay awake at night thinking about how unfair this all is, then the problem is not the disparity but the illness of discontent and envy in *my* soul. I have become ungrateful. What is true for us as individual Christians is also true for us when we consider the disparities in our world. Before we join the noisy choruses singing about unfairness in our society and add to the hostility generated against banks, insurance companies, oil companies, pharmaceutical firms, doctors, etc., we should pause to note that "fairness" is often a code word used by those who want to manipulate feelings of envy and resentment into a political force. From a theological perspective, we need to see that it can also be evidence of a clenched fist raised in anger against God and his providence. Nothing illustrates this as well as the attack on "privilege."

Let me introduce the question of privilege with that wise theologian, Charles Schulz, creator of the comic strip *Peanuts*, and his treatment of privilege (and election) in a four-panel strip. In the first panel, Snoopy is sitting watching Charley Brown saunter by and muses: "I wonder why some of us were born dogs while others were born people . . ." In the second Snoopy probes deeper: "Is it just pure chance, or what is it?" In the third one, as Linus marches past in the opposite direction, the injustice of it all sinks in: "Somehow the whole thing doesn't seem very fair." And in the final panel Snoopy is trotting off alone with the surprising conclusion: "Why should *I* have been the lucky one." Ah, yes—it's a dog's life all right.

This cartoon always comes to mind when I come across challenges to the very notion of privilege. During the summer of 2011, a West Michigan pastor, Rob Bell of Mars Hill Bible Church, generated massive media coverage thanks to the publication of his book *Love Wins*. Bell challenged the "privilege" of God's grace to particular people (Reformed people would say "the elect") as not being fair. Why should someone's eternal destiny depend on missionaries coming with the gospel about Jesus and saying the right words about Jesus? "What if," Bell wonders out loud, "the missionary's car has a flat tire?" Bell's "better" answer is a more inclusive model of God's love "winning." Though it sounds like universalism, Bell studiously avoids the term, and it is not my desire here to dismiss him because of it. Instead I want to ask why advantage or privilege should be considered some kind of problem to be overcome.

If I am born into a happy Christian family, nurtured in the faith, and grow up to be a disciple of Jesus, then my circumstances spiritually privilege me over a child born in India to Hindu parents. I can respond to this in one of two ways: (1) consider the privilege as a gift of God's providence, one of the means of his sovereign grace, and be grateful; or, (2) think that the privilege is unfair, feel some measure of guilt for it, and pursue ways to level the playing field. Either response, of course, could lead one to obey our Lord's missionary call to share the gospel. But it makes a difference whether our missionary impulse is fueled by gratitude or guilt. In the former we share of our abundant gift; in the latter we might be led to disparage the gift we have been given. In that case, even if we do not intend it, our ingratitude dishonors the Giver who has providentially made the gift possible and bestowed it on us.

Perhaps the second response seems far-fetched; why would one not be grateful for the privilege of salvation? Yet, this is exactly the logic behind affluent Christians in the West denouncing, in the name of biblical prophecy, the very democratic, free-market economies that have materially blessed them. Consider, for example, the call of the Accra Confession for Reformed Christians to "acknowledge the complicity and guilt of those who consciously or unconsciously benefit from the current neoliberal economic global system" and "confess our sin in misusing creation and failing to play our role as stewards and companions of nature." Whatever one makes of this "confession," it is clearly fueled by guilt and hostility to the free-market economic order, which is judged harshly because it produces such unfair results.

But, against what or whom is this accusation addressed? According to Thomas Sowell in *The Quest for Cosmic Justice*, in which he quotes from and summarizes the work of Austrian economist Friedrich Hayek, the complaint only makes sense as a protest against God. Hayek observed that "the manner in which the benefits and burdens are apportioned by the market mechanism would in many instances have to be regarded as very unjust *if* it were the result of a deliberate allocation to a particular people." *If!* Sowell notes that "[t]he only reason [Hayek] did not regard it as unjust was because 'the particulars of a spontaneous order cannot be just or unjust.'" There is no personal actor or intentionality in a market process leading to the democratic capitalist order that is our present reality. In Hayek's words: "Nature can be neither just nor unjust. Only if we mean to blame a personal creator does it make sense to describe it as unjust that somebody has been born with a physical defect, or been stricken with a disease, or has suffered the loss of a loved one" (4). The complaint is against God!

Now, challenging the fairness of God's providence and fostering guilt about God's good gifts to us ought to trouble all Christians. We need to pause long and hard before we join the chorus of ecclesiastical jeremiads against the unfairness of the global market economy. To see how troubling this accusation is, let's look more closely at the characteristic response to the obvious inequities in the world summarized by the term *social justice*.

The expression "social justice" entered into Roman Catholic social teaching in 1931 when Pope Pius XI commemorated the fortieth anniversary of Leo XIII's encyclical "On the Condition of Workers" (*Rerum Novarum*) with his own encyclical, "On Reconstructing the Social Order" (*Quadragesimo Anno*). Concern about the "common good" was the focus of the encyclical. Taking his point of departure from his predecessor's words—"However the earth may be apportioned among private owners, it does not cease to serve the *common interests of all*" (*Rerum Novarum*, § 40, emphasis added)—the pope introduced the term "social justice" as the norm for distribution of property and wealth that serves "the common good of society" (*Quadragesimo Anno*, §§ 56–57; for more on these encyclicals, see Jean-Yves Calvez and Jacques Perrin, *The Church and Social Justice: The Social Teaching of the Popes from Leo XIII to Pius XII [1878–1958]*). "Social justice" is simply another term for "the common good," or what the Roman Catholic tradition of moral teaching used to call "legal justice," the broad, general, and objective norm covering all human relationships. The key principle of legal justice is "giving to each its proper due." Social justice did not mean then what it has come to mean today.

What is this new understanding of social justice? We gain clarity when we use Thomas Sowell's preferred term "cosmic justice." Whereas traditional justice is about unbiased and fair *processes* (in legal terms, *due process*), no matter what the outcome, cosmic justice is driven by a distress about unequal *outcomes*. "Playing by the same rules" is not enough when the results reflect disparities that are morally troubling to some. "Through no fault of their own" is a key phrase in the pursuit of cosmic justice:

> Implicit in much discussion of a need to rectify social inequities is the notion that some segments of society, *through no fault of their own*, lack things which others receive as windfall gains, *through no virtue of their own*. (*Quest for Cosmic Justice*, 13, emphasis added)

The remedy to this unfairness is to "level the playing field" in one way or the other. Sowell's main objection against such an expanded notion of justice is that it attempts to put humans in the place of God: "We do not have the omniscience to know . . ." (18). Furthermore, "the question is not what we would do if we were God on the first day of Creation or how we would judge souls if we were God on Judgment Day. The question is: What lies within our knowledge and control, given that we are only human, with all the severe limitations which that implies?" (21).

Even if we could know who are deprived "through no fault of their own" and who are blessed "through no virtue of their own," what are we to do about it and what are the unintended consequences of our remedies? Since some form of coercive redistribution is usually called for, what is the cost to human liberty? If "playing by the rules" yields results that are "unfair," won't using the coercive power of the state to redistribute wealth effectively destroy the important moral nexus between human action and consequences? When someone's earnings and profits are seen not as just deserts for work performed but as a "windfall" gain, do we not risk turning the entire economic realm into a lottery where the state picks winners and losers? Is there any difference between government redistribution with no thought to merit and a lottery? In both cases the beneficiaries did not "earn" their wages and might even be willing to gamble that they could avoid work and "get lucky." Redistribution creates people with incentives to become dependent on the lottery of state benefits (20–25).

Here we need to return to the distinction made in chapter 3 between a spontaneous, organic order and a designed, constructed, or organized order. The success of the latter is measured by clear objectives and measurable outcomes. An organization created to provide housing for poor people can count the number of homes built, the number of families serviced, and so forth. It may set its goals too high and be disappointed or set them too low and be pleasantly surprised. In either case, the measurement is clear and the participants in the organization have defined responsibilities that can be assessed. Spontaneous, organic orders such as the market are quite different. The outcome of a market's operation cannot be known in advance because, although the individual actors have their own goals, there is no coordinated, overall plan that governs it. There is no *ultimate* measurable goal by which all participants should be judged. Consequently, each of the two orders is governed by a different kind of justice. A constructed order meets the standard of justice when its participants are appropriately rewarded for doing their assigned tasks. They receive their just deserts. The example of a school comes to mind. A school is a made order, designed and organized to produce literate, skilled, productive citizens. In each of its parts, justice is done when a student receives the appropriate grade for work done, a B+ for B+ work and a C- for C- work.

Justice in spontaneous or organic orders such as the market is different. Arnoud Pellissier-Tanon and José Moreira identify what differentiates these differing orders: "In the grown order, the coordination of individual actions depends on the *reliability of behavior*" ("Can Social Justice Be Achieved?" *Journal of Markets and Morality*, 147, emphasis added). Justice is served when promises are kept, contracts are honored, goods and services are of high quality, workers provide an honest day's labor and are rewarded with a fair wage, and so forth. Predictability, trust, consistency, and integrity are crucial. According to Hayek, the term *social justice* is properly applied to constructed orders and simply means that "society treats individuals according to their deserts" (Quoted in Pellissier-Tanon and Moreira, "Can Social Justice Be Achieved?" 147). In the same way that it would be wrong to apply a standard of equality to a school (in the name of "fairness" or enhancing self-esteem, give every student an A), it is also meaningless to apply the term *social justice* to the results of the market. Pellissier-Tanon and Moreira again quote Hayek:

> In a free society in which the position of the different individuals and groups is not the result of anybody's design—or could, within such a society, be altered in accordance with a generally applicable principle—the differences in reward simply cannot meaningfully be described as just or unjust. (Ibid.)

This leads us to what will seem to many to be a scandalizing conclusion in the words of French philosopher Bertrand de Jouvenel: "It is impossible to establish a just social order" (Quoted in Pellissier-Tanon and Moreira, "Can Social Justice Be Achieved?" 150). This is such a startling conclusion that it requires some explanation. We can speak positively about societies that are *more or less* just depending on the degree to which a spirit of justice and fairness pervades all human actions and a legal structure seeks as much as possible to embody equal treatment before the law. By this criterion some societies are more just than others even though none is perfectly just. What we are rejecting is the possibility of a "just social order" understood as one where there is no inequality, where no one is ever harmed, where a full life is guaranteed for everyone. In other words, what we are rejecting is the possibility of achieving the fullness of the kingdom of God on earth through our efforts. Christians who confidently live in the hope of bodily resurrection and the renewal of all things in the consummation should never permit their vision to be disturbed and distorted by such utopian dreaming. One of the great scandals of our times is the eagerness with which far too many in the modern church are willing to sell their soul to such dreaming.

There are many issues I have introduced in this chapter and not developed further. In conclusion, I want to call attention to some serious doctrinal/theological problems attending the antimarket attitudes and rhetoric emanating from the mainline churches' social justice offices. The hostility to the market and the prosperity it has produced is, as I have said, a mark of ingratitude, a refusal to give thanks to the Giver for his gifts. Ingratitude also fuels envy, one of the capital sins. Lord Peter Bauer in a chapter title once characterized the posturing of the churches on economics as "Ecclesiastical Economics: Envy Legitimized." "Envy," Bauer said, "is traditionally one of the seven deadly sins. Vocal modern clerical opinion endows it with moral legitimacy and intellectual respectability" (Quoted in *Is Capitalism Christian?* ed. Franky Schaeffer, 327). At the very least, this ought to give us pause; is it possible that our zeal for social justice encourages deadly sin? And is it not the church's task to counter deadly sin rather than contribute to it?

In connection with this, we also need to take seriously the way in which a passion for equality runs the risk of rebelling against God's providence. The inequities of today were more than matched by those of late nineteenth-century Europe and America. Thanks to the Industrial Revolution and the resultant dislocation of working people from rural areas into the urban centers of Europe as cottage industries gave way to "factory" production, the misery of the working poor was on every thinking Christian's radar as "the social question." Dutch Reformed Christians held their First Christian Social Congress in Amsterdam on November 9–12, 1891, and both of the giants of Dutch neo-Calvinism, Abraham Kuyper and Herman Bavinck, played major roles. Kuyper's address mentioned in chapter 1 ("The Social Question and the Christian Religion," Eng. trans. of its title, later published as *The Problem of Poverty*) is the more famous of the two, but Bavinck's deserves equal attention for its solid biblical grounding and theological depth as its lengthy title suggests ("General Biblical Principles and the Relevance of Concrete Mosaic Law for the Social Question Today"). Among other things, Bavinck in his address claimed that inequalities are not the consequence of the fall but a given of the good creation: "Even the existence of inequalities among people is rooted in creation, that is to say, in God's will, and serves precisely to make possible humanity's earthly task." Bavinck is simply acknowledging that individuals and nations do not have equal access to the gifts and resources of creation. Some individuals are smarter and more gifted than others, have greater opportunities, and enjoy more favorable circumstances. Similarly, some nations have an abundance of natural resources, access to rivers and oceans to facilitate trade, and climates that are amenable to work, while others have less. Africa is endowed with far greater resources than Iceland or Japan, and neither of the latter two have the resources of oil that Saudi Arabia does. Landlocked Switzerland did not start out with any economic privileges or advantages over, let's say, Portugal. Providence's bounties are not equally distributed. And still what we see today are prosperous nations such as Japan, Malaysia, South Korea, and even the rock island of Hong Kong, while most of the vast African continent—with a few notable exceptions such as South Africa—languishes in varying degrees of poverty. What we do with what we have is crucial, and the outcomes we see over generations and centuries could never have been designed or predicted in advance. Global judgments about unfairness, along with grand schemes to "fix" things, are attempts by finite and fallible human actors to play the role of God.

And then there is the matter of guilt. Should our appropriate compassion for the wretched of this world lead to feelings of guilt? I do not claim apodictic certainty about this, but I do wonder whether or not this reflects a telling instance of transference for liberal Christianity. Here is H. Richard Niebuhr's famous definition of liberal Protestantism: "A God without wrath brought men without sin into a kingdom without judgment through the ministrations of a Christ without a cross" (*The Kingdom of God in America*, 198). Liberal Christianity rejects original sin and will have nothing to do with Christ's substitutionary atonement as the payment for humanity's guilt. The problem, however, is that we *are* guilty before God and our guilt cannot be wished away. Deep down people know this and have to deal with it. Is it possible that, having eliminated our solidarity in Adam's sin and Christ's obedient sacrifice as the answer to our guilt, liberal Christianity has turned to social guilt as a substitute? "We are guilty—of unfairly benefitting from an unjust world-system." If so, is it also possible that calling Western Christians to confess the guilt of their participation in structures of injustice, and atoning by working tirelessly on behalf of the world's poor, is what theologians would call a new soteriology, a new doctrine of salvation, as the answer to misplaced and projected guilt? Are we saved by joining God in his identification with the marginalized and oppressed? This would be, we should note, a salvation by works and not by grace alone.

I offer these last few pages not as an accusation but as a call for further discussion. Good intentions for the poor are no substitute for disciplined theological reflection, especially when those intentions open us up to sins of ingratitude, pride, envy, and works-righteousness.

At the close of this lengthy chapter, I am keenly aware that I have done little more than clear away some of the underbrush of misunderstanding and downright error so that we can see the forest of the market more clearly. I am also aware that I have not adequately answered all the appropriate and important questions that flow from our compassionate and weary hearts about the wretched of the earth. Our obligations to the poor are of sufficient importance to warrant an entire chapter, and it is to that we now turn.

Discussion Questions

1. Whether we always feel it or not, the author and readers of this book need to be ranked among the affluent of this world; we all have more than we absolutely need for basic subsistence. Does this make you feel guilty? Should it? If it makes you grateful instead, how do you avoid becoming indifferent to the misery of the poor?

2. How do you respond to someone who comes to you with the claim that only those who follow Jesus' advice to the rich young ruler to "go, sell what you possess and give to the poor" can be counted as true followers of Jesus?

For Further Reading

Accra Confession. Adopted by delegates of the World Alliance of Reformed Churches, 24th General Council, Accra, Ghana (2004). Available at http://www.wcrc.ch/node/469.

Baeur, P. T. "Ecclesiastical Economics: Envy Legitimized." Chap. 15 in *Is Capitalism Christian?* Edited by Franky Schaeffer. Westchester, IL: Crossway, 1985.

Bell, Daniel. *The Cultural Contradictions of Capitalism.* 20th anniversary ed. New York: Basic Books, 1996.

Calvez, Jean-Yves, and Jacques Perrin. *The Church and Social Justice: The Social Teaching of the Popes from Leo XIII to Pius XII (1878–1958).* Translated by J. R. Kirwan. Chicago: Henry Regnery, 1961. This book includes all of the social encyclicals represented, except *Laborem Exercens* or *Centesimus Annus* or any encyclical published after 1961. Citations of encyclicals prior to 1961 and to *Centesimus*

Annus in chapter 8, however, are to the versions on the Vatican Web site, http://www.vatican.va/.

Friedman, Milton, and Rose Friedman. *Free to Choose: A Personal Statement.* New York: Harcourt Brace Jovanovich, 1980.

Levinson, Marc. *The Great A&P and the Struggle for Small Business in America.* New York: Hill and Wang, 2013.

McIntyre, Douglas A., Samuel Weigley, Alexander E. M. Hess, and Michael B. Sauter. "Eight Retailers That Will Close the Most Stores." 24/7 Wall St., January 29, 2013. http://247wallst.com/special-report/2013/01/29/eight-retailers-that-will-close-the-most-stores/.

Niebuhr, H. Richard. *The Kingdom of God in America.* Middletown, CT: Wesleyan University Press, 1988. First published in 1937.

Pellissier-Tanon, Arnoud, and José Moreira. "Can Social Justice Be Achieved?" *Journal of Markets and Morality* 10, no. 1 (Spring 2007): 143–55. http://www.marketsandmorality.com/index.php/mandm/article/view/266/257.

Schulz, David P. "Top 100 Retailers." *STORES* magazine, July 2013. http://www.stores.org/STORES%20Magazine%20July%202013/top-100-retailers.

Sowell, Thomas. *The Quest for Cosmic Justice.* New York: Free Press, 1999.

Weiser, Jay, "The Big Store: The Mythology of Small Business Meets a Retailing Giant." Review of *The Great A&P and the Struggle for Small Business in America* by Marc Levinson, *The Weekly Standard,* April 29, 2013, 33–35. http://www.weeklystandard.com/articles/big-store_718089.html.

Wolterstorff, Nicholas. *Until Justice and Peace Embrace: The Kuyper Lectures for 1981 Delivered at the Free University of Amsterdam.* Grand Rapids: Eerdmans, 1983.

"The Poor You Will Always Have with You"

Opportunity, Obligation, and Responsibility

The soul of the sluggard craves and gets nothing, while the soul of the diligent is richly supplied.
Proverbs 13:4

Give me neither poverty nor riches; feed me with the food that is needful for me, lest I be full and deny you and say, "Who is the Lord?" or lest I be poor and steal and profane the name of my God.
Agur's prayer, Proverbs 30:8–9

The community which has neither poverty nor riches will always have the noblest principles.
Plato

Resolve not to be poor: whatever you have, spend less. Poverty is a great enemy to human happiness; it certainly destroys liberty, and it makes some virtues impracticable, and others extremely difficult.
Samuel Johnson

He who is not capable of enduring poverty is not capable of being free.
Victor Hugo

Being unwanted, unloved, uncared for, forgotten by everybody, I think that is a much greater hunger, a much greater poverty than the person who has nothing to eat.
Mother Teresa

The title of this chapter—taken from Matthew 26:11 (NIV; par. Mark 14:7; John 12:8)—may be the best known and most frequently quoted words of our Lord Jesus Christ on the subject of poverty. The only possible rival is the familiar passage from the Sermon on the Mount: "Blessed are the poor [in spirit]" (Matt. 5:3; par. Luke 6:20). The verse from Deuteronomy that Jesus is quoting—"There will always be poor people in the land" (Deut. 15:11a NIV)—comes in a passage explaining the Sabbath-year provision when God commands the people of Israel to cancel and forgive the debts of fellow Israelites. Included in the passage is a comment that suggests the Sabbath-year provision should be extraordinary and not needed very often: "However, there need be no poor people among you, for in the land the LORD your God is giving you to possess as an inheritance, he will richly bless you, if only you fully obey the LORD your God" (Deut. 15:4–5a NIV).

This startling juxtaposition of ideas in the passages cited from Deuteronomy—"there *need* be no poor people among you" but "there *will* always be poor people"—is a valuable caution that we not misuse the words of Jesus for our own ideological purposes. This happens all too often; two of our Lord's parables are particularly susceptible to abuse. The parable of the householder and the workers in the vineyard (Matt. 20:1–16) is frequently misapplied to defend socialist equalizing schemes of redistribution. After all, everyone receives the same pay at the end of the day whether they have worked from sunrise or only for one hour. "Stop your grumbling!" On the other side of the political spectrum, the parable of the talents (Matt. 25:14–30) has been used to make the opposite point—hard work should be rewarded even if it results in greater inequality. The single "talent" is taken from the lazy, unproductive servant and given to the most productive one. Let us be clear: neither parable has anything to do with economics or economic systems; the economy is a *simile* for the kingdom of God! In the former parable, the economic dynamic is a sign of God's generous grace; in the latter, a warning not to squander by inactivity the precious gifts of the kingdom. Both teachings of course are applicable to the Christian life of discipleship, including our economic life; our stewardship of God's gifts of grace is not limited to but also includes our possessions.

Let's now consider possible misapplications of Jesus' response—"the poor you will always have with you"—to the complaint that the "precious ointment" poured out on him before his death "could have been sold for a large sum and given to the poor" (Matt. 26:9; par. Mark 14:5; John 12:5). Is it illegitimate, for example, to use this text as a preemptive warning against utopian dreaming about "eradicating all poverty by . . . (fill in the blank)"? Not entirely, but it would be a *secondary* inference that runs the risk of encouraging a mood resignation that just gives up on any concern for the poor. After all, the poor will always be there. Ho hum. This would directly contradict the primary intention of our Lord's words and lead us to a sinful indifference. The point of Jesus' observation about the poor always being there is that their presence gives *us* untold opportunity as well as ongoing obligation to aid the needy. Jesus will not be with them much longer; the woman's anointing of him "for his burial" is thus appropriate. *But*—the poor will be your neighbors *always*. That this is our Lord's intention is underscored by the words in the Deuteronomy text that immediately follow the observation about there always being poor people in the land: "Therefore I command you to be openhanded toward your fellow Israelites who are poor and needy in your land" (Deut. 15:11b NIV). Even if this were the only reference in Scripture to our obligation for the poor, it would be enough to challenge our sinful evasions of responsibility for the poor living in our midst. Of course there is much more in Scripture to bolster this point—a partial list includes Leviticus 19:10; 23:22; Luke 4:18, 14:13; Acts 9:36; Galatians 2:10; James 2—and it should be granted without dispute that there is a solemn moral obligation for those who claim to be God's people, who claim to have been redeemed from bondage, to demonstrate compassionate generosity to the poor. In other words, the body of Christ has an indisputable responsibility toward the poor.

How does this moral obligation translate into concrete strategy and action? We examined the broader issue of how to apply biblical teaching to economics in chapter 1 and will only provide a brief summary statement here. It is a mistake, we said, to go to the Bible to find scientific information about the world or about human life in society, including economics. The Bible is a *spiritual* resource, directing us to God and to being reconciled with God. It is a word of renewal and redirection for our *life in creation*, a life that precedes our redemption. Following the lead of Dutch Reformed theologian Herman Bavinck, we said that it was better to speak of certain key biblical *principles* relevant for economics than to speak of a "biblical economics." The best we can do is to evaluate particular economic systems as being more or less *consistent with biblical teaching*. The key biblical teaching for economic life, we proposed, was the doctrine that all human beings are created in the image of God and therefore must be treated with dignity as morally responsible individuals. Liberty, therefore, must be primary in any evaluation of an economic system. We also noted that the Bible's wisdom literature, the prudential advice based on experience of life in God's creation, contains much that is applicable to our work, our business, and our consumption.

Applying this to the particular question of "the poor" leads to the following propositions, which will be unpacked in the remainder of this chapter:

1. The "poor" must be considered and treated as image bearers of God, that is to say, as free, morally responsible agents.

2. The final goal of poverty alleviation is the restoration of opportunity for poor people to fulfill their calling as God's image bearers.

3. The reality of poverty in our world places specific obligations upon all Christians for showing mercy in our various capacities as

   * neighbors,

   * church members,

   * citizens, and

   * those who are wealthy.

The "Poor" Bear the Image of God

Since they are image bearers of God, the poor share responsibility for their poverty and for overcoming it. Undoubtedly, this claim will arouse fierce protest from those who will judge that this only "blames the victim" for their victimization. That is not my intention. I make the claim because I believe it is essential to "disaggregate" the poor; there is no one single, simple undifferentiated mass of people in a particular society that we can lump together as the "poor." Admittedly, some of the distinctions that have been made—such as between "deserving" poor and "undeserving" poor—are singularly unhelpful, even offensive. That being said, we do need to make a distinction between voluntary poverty (chosen by graduate students, for example) and the involuntary poverty that results from loss of job and income, illness, or disability. But, even then, involuntary poverty does not make anyone a "victim" in the sense that one is so helpless as to justify passivity about one's situation. Poor people are God's image bearers, and the mantle of victimhood does not rest well on the shoulders of those who are called to image God. This does not mean that those who are not poor have no responsibilities or obligation to provide assistance to the weakest and neediest among us, and we will get to that in due time. My initial concern here is to elevate even the poor to the highest position of human dignity and moral responsibility.

If the first thing we need to affirm is that the poor are image bearers of God, and that to be an image bearer is to be a responsive and responsible person, the second thing we need to point out is that the poor are also sinners. The Christian doctrine of original sin teaches that all people are by nature sinners: "For all have sinned and fall short of the glory of God" (Rom. 3:23). This truth, however, does not absolve the sinner from the guilt produced by specific acts of sin; even sinners are accountable for their sins. Similarly, it is a mistake to absolve the "poor" altogether from the sins that result in poverty *for some*. The wisdom literature of the Bible suggests that laziness and profligacy result in poverty. We are instructed to live disciplined lives and avoid repetitive use of the slumber buttons on our alarm clocks. "Poverty and disgrace come to him who ignores instruction, but whoever heeds reproof is honored" (Prov. 13:18). Diligence and hard work are praised in that delightful paean of praise to the ant in Proverbs 6:6–11:

> Go to the ant, O sluggard;
>   consider her ways, and be wise.
> Without having any chief,
>   officer, or ruler,
> she prepares her bread in summer
>   and gathers her food in harvest.
> How long will you lie there, O sluggard?
>   When will you arise from your sleep?
> A little sleep, a little slumber,
>   a little folding of the hands to rest,
> and poverty will come upon you like a robber,
>   and want like an armed man.

In addition, there are warnings against trying to borrow our way to happiness: "The rich rules over the poor, and the borrower is the slave of the lender" (Prov. 22:7). Then, there are those warnings against get-rich-quick schemes and dreaming about winning the lottery as substitutes for hard work: "The plans of the diligent lead surely to abundance, but everyone who is hasty comes only to poverty" (Prov. 21:5). "Whoever works his land will have plenty of bread, but he who follows worthless pursuits lacks sense" (Prov. 12:11).

Having said this, it must also be said that as we contemplate the masses of poor people in the world, it would be equally immoral for us to judge them all as lazy or profligate or lacking in other important character traits. Recall our discussion in chapter 5 about the "dead capital" in the developing countries of the world where human creativity and entrepreneurship and hard work are not able to provide the breakthroughs needed for broader human flourishing. Laziness and unwillingness to work are not the problem there; absence of a political-legal framework that guarantees property rights is the problem. In addition, there are victims of oppression, tyranny, disease, and disability, all of whom may not have the physical ability or, even with physical ability, lack all opportunity to significantly rise above their impoverished state. That is precisely the point: it is a serious failure of understanding and imagination for ethicists, analysts, and policy makers not to make important distinctions among the poor and attempt a one-size-fits-all approach to poverty alleviation.

A 1985 study titled *Gaining Ground: New Approaches to Poverty and Dependency* by the Ethics and Public Policy Center claimed that, assuming a noncatastrophic situation where work is available, there were at least three things that a healthy, able-bodied adult poor person can do that would significantly lower rates of poverty in America: (1) *stay in school*, (2) *get a job and keep it*, and (3) *get married and stay married*. These are demanding tasks, especially for those who grow up in dysfunctional homes and communities.

Difficult, yes, but not impossibly heroic. The three criteria suggested are linked together in terms of biblical morality and sociological wisdom. Education provides both the discipline and skills that are needed in the workplace; families provide the context within which such discipline is nurtured and, in the case of married people, the reason for work in order to provide for one's own. Pope John Paul II, in his encyclical *Laborem Exercens* ("On Human Work"), describes the mutuality this way:

> Work constitutes a foundation for the formation of *family life*, which is a natural right and something that man is called to. These two spheres of values—one linked to work and the other consequent on the family nature of human life—must be properly united and must properly permeate each other. In a way, work is a condition for making it possible to found a family, since the family requires the means of subsistence which man normally gains through work. Work and industriousness also influence the whole *process of education* in the family, for the very reason that everyone "becomes a human being" through, among other things, work, and becoming a human being is precisely the main purpose of the whole process of education. Obviously, two aspects of work in a sense come into play here: the one making family life and its upkeep possible, and the other making possible the achievement of the purposes of the family, especially education. . . . These two aspects of work are linked to one another and are mutually complementary. . . . (§ 10; see Vatican Web site)

This acknowledgement that certain attitudes, habits, disciplines, and behaviors are essential to combat endemic poverty is all too often ignored by those who benefit politically by publicly posturing as the "saviors of the poor." That Christians also fall into this trap of anointing themselves as the poor's "saviors" is nothing short of scandalous. The poor have the same Savior as the rich, and that Savior died on a cross and rose from the dead more than two thousand years ago.

In this connection, highlighting our conviction about the universality of sin also means that we must resist isolating one group or class as especially sinful while downplaying or exempting the sin in others. We do that when we consider the industrious and wealthy as virtuous and the poor as indolent and lazy, attributing poverty simply to sinful behavior by the poor. This ignores the stern warnings of Scripture against the evil rich whose wealth is the fruit of oppression (Amos 5:11–12; James 5:1–6). In our day, the opposite practice is as common: demonizing people of wealth and romantically bestowing privileged virtue on the poor simply because they are poor. This is defended by claiming that "God is on the side of the poor" without providing any subtlety of nuance or qualification. Not only does this contradict Scripture's teaching that all are sinners, without exception, it also ignores the lessons of history about what happens when the "virtuous poor" take hold of the reins of power after the liberation provided by the revolution. Abraham Kuyper was aware of this more than a hundred years ago. Commenting on the frequent failure of magistrates to defend the cause of the weak and poor and instead to use their power against them, he noted: "This was not because the stronger class was more evil at heart than the weaker, for no sooner did a man from the lower class rise to the top than he in his turn took part just as harshly—yes, even more harshly—in the wicked oppression of those who were members of his own former class" (*The Problem of Poverty*, 33). We who have survived the twentieth century know this tragedy all too well: revolutions devour their own children; when the oppressed throw off the yoke of their bondage they become bondsmen themselves.

Let me summarize the point I am trying to make in the preceding section: the poor are image bearers of God, and our response to the staggering offense of poverty in our world must honor them as responsible moral subjects. This is exactly the point made by Pope Francis (then Cardinal Bergoglio) in a September 2009 presentation "Las Deudas Sociales" (Social Debts/ Obligations):

> [W]e cannot truly respond to the challenge of eradicating exclusion and poverty if the poor continue to be objects, targets of action by the state and other organizations in a paternalistic and aid-based sense (*asistencialista*), instead of subjects, [in an environment] where the state and society create social conditions that promote and safeguard their rights and allow them to build their own destiny. (Quoted in Michael Matheson Miller, "Street Smarts," *The American Spectator*, March 3, 2013)

Amen!

Restoring Opportunity, Creating Wealth

In *Rich Christians in an Age of Hunger* Ron Sider tells the allegorical story of a group of Christians who lived in a small village at the foot of a mountain whose steep winding road along dangerous precipices without guardrails resulted in numerous accidents with serious injuries. Moved by compassion for the suffering, they decided to purchase an ambulance, took turns volunteering as paramedics, and drove injured people in the ambulance to the hospital in the next village. One day a visitor came to town and asked why the villagers didn't close the road and build a tunnel to prevent accidents rather than merely respond with works of mercy (219–20). My own application does not precisely follow Sider's road, but the allegory rightly points to the limits of charity, necessary as it is in emergencies. When it comes to the poor and those who are suffering, charity and mercy to address the immediacies of their needy circumstances, whether it be food, clothing, shelter, or medical attention, are stopgap measures and not long-term remedies.

That is precisely the point of the Old Testament Sabbath and Jubilee legislation. Debt cancellation and return of land to the family whose inheritance it was did not represent charity or mercy, nor, we should hasten to add, were they a matter of redistributing wealth per se but a restoration of *opportunity to create wealth*. This is clear from the stipulation that the value of the land to be bought and sold was not its intrinsic worth as real estate but the number of harvests available from it until the year of Jubilee (Lev. 25:14–17). Crops and harvests do not just happen; they require work and husbandry. Seed must be sown, weeds pulled, fields harvested and threshed, and grain milled. In the process of restoration, obligations are also placed on those who are needy. When people get new opportunities they must work hard to make the most of them. Hence the instruction of the apostle Paul follows a similar pattern: "If anyone is not willing to work, let him not eat" (2 Thess. 3:10). And, alternatively, "A slack hand causes poverty, but the hand of the diligent makes rich" (Prov. 10:4).

This suggests that while poor people may have a "right" to *opportunities* that will enable them to escape poverty, and a right of claim (property) to the fruits of their labors (confirmed by the commandment "thou shalt not steal"), this does not translate into a *right* to the fruit of another's labor. The wealthy are called to share of their abundance, but this is in Scripture a matter of voluntary charity. The Bible simply does not call for redistribution from the wealthy to the poor as its answer to the problem of poverty. Rather it places responsibilities and obligations on all of us, including the poor themselves. For the Old Testament Israelite, getting out of poverty required the restoration of opportunity made possible by a return to ancestral property. Depending on circumstances, things are much more complicated for us today.

In the case of someone who, let's say, loses a job with no prospects of returning to it because the company has moved overseas or gone bankrupt, restored opportunity may include a willingness to relocate, furthering one's education or skill development, and even a willingness to accept a "lesser" job with lower pay and benefits. None of this is easy, but, again, it is not impossible for an able-bodied person. For inner-city youth who grow up in seriously dysfunctional families, suffer through inferior schools, and never develop the moral-cultural habits needed to thrive in the world of work, the challenges and difficulties rise exponentially.

Whatever the situation in which the poor find themselves, there is only one way to lift the poor out of poverty. If someone who is poor today is to have any chance of not being poor tomorrow, he or she must have *opportunity* to work and receive the just deserts of honest labor. This is the only way we honor people as image bearers of God, as *cocreators* with God. In other words, the poor must be given opportunity *to create wealth*. Put that way, we can see what is so troublingly wrong about using coercive redistribution as the primary means of alleviating poverty. Redistribution assumes that wealth is a given and that it is only a matter of cutting up the existing pie. Poverty is caused by greedy people who take more than their fair share. But that is to turn things on their head; it fails to ask how the wealth pie was created in the first place and by whom. Wealth is created because of the *value* that God and human beings place on things. Oil underneath the Arabian sand or diamonds deep in the Transvaal earth are just "gunk" and "hard rocks" until human labor and use give them value. For the poor to rise up from their poverty they must join the company of those who *use* the earth's resources.

In this connection, we need to counter a current misunderstanding of the notion of "stewardship." The biblical mandate for responsible stewardship of creation is clear: "The LORD God took the man and put him in the garden of Eden to work it and *keep it* [i.e., *take care of it*]" (Gen. 2:15, emphasis added). The laws God gave to Israel in the books of Moses underscore this. The value of land and even of fruit-bearing trees is in their crops; land must regularly lie fallow to prevent over-farming; even nesting birds are to be protected from the harvester's scythe. The productivity of the field and trees must be protected for the sake of the generations yet to come. Today, however, some who are passionate about the environment seem to believe that stewardship means leaving nature in its pristine condition untouched and unaffected by human hands. The North American Coalition for Christianity and Ecology (NACCE) spoke in a newsletter of activity in which people "relentlessly oppress the Earth and violate the integrity of creation" as a sin, where "sin" was defined as refusing "to act in the image of God." A 1991 "Statement by Religious Leaders at the Summit on Environment," issued by two dozen Jewish, Protestant, Catholic, and Native American representatives, insists that "we must maintain [the Earth's environment] as we received it."

This reduction of the good biblical notion of stewardship to maintaining creation in the pristine character of government-controlled nature preserves cannot be right. It often seems to escape spokespersons for the environmental movement that the only way out of poverty is creative and improved human utilization of creation's resources. Protestors against the use of fossil fuels or nuclear power to provide electricity and heat in our temperate or cold northern hemisphere climates tend to forget that the earlier method of keeping warm by each social unit having its own fire fueled by wood or coal is far less environmentally friendly. If California's environmental purity ends up with Californians in the cold and dark because they lack the nuclear and other power plants needed to meet energy demands, it is not only the wealthy dot-com entrepreneurs in Silicon Valley or the Rodeo Drive shopping residents of Beverly Hills who get hit, but also the poor children in Oakland or West Los Angeles. Sometimes extremist environmental policies end up particularly harming the poor because they negate our human calling to use the resources entrusted to us by the Creator to better the condition of us all. We need the liberty to make responsible use of the world's resources in the most productive and efficient manner possible to benefit everyone. We cannot help the poor escape material poverty *without using creation's riches*. And the only way to truly *lift the poor* is to provide them with the opportunity to join other fellow image bearers in being responsive, responsible, productive members of society. We need to pursue policies that encourage the poor to become active image bearers of God.

The Obligation of Charity

Before poor people can stand on their own feet, they need to be kept alive. Here we come to the second dimension of the image of God—we are social or communal creatures. When we consider the poor, not only is our "dominion over creation" in play—our capacity for using earth's resources to create wealth—but so is our obligation to love our neighbor. From the abundance of biblical testimony to the central importance of neighbor-love, I want to focus on the conclusion to the apostle Paul's great hymn to love in 1 Corinthians 13: "but the greatest of these is love" (v. 13). For reasons that will become apparent, I personally retain a fondness for the King James Version: "but the greatest of these is charity."

It is not our loss of facility in Elizabethan English that has led to a virtual disappearance of the word *charity* in our time, at least as a positive notion. Charity is now frequently seen as something demeaning, a patronizing gesture that incubates a double sin: it creates proud and arrogant givers along with humiliated, resentful receivers. Social Gospel theologian Walter Rauschenbusch gave voice to a new concern a century ago when he contrasted charity with justice. "The fault in our modern charity," he wrote, "is that love is made to do the work of justice, an upside-down arrangement that makes even the simple precepts of Jesus appear unwise and impracticable. Such masses of poverty as our great cities possess have not been created by private fault or misfortune but by social injustice, and therefore of course private charity cannot cope with it, but social justice must put a stop to its production." To this Rauschenbusch added, "Charity can never be more than supplementary to justice." The proper order, according to Rauschenbusch? "Public justice and then private charity, that is the only true order" (*Righteousness of the Kingdom*, 228–29).

My own view is that the proper order is exactly the other way around. Charity or love precedes "social justice" when it comes to the poor among us. In part I want to reverse the order because I believe that Rauschenbusch's diagnosis and remedy are equally flawed. Since I have already covered this territory earlier in chapters 1 and 5, I will only summarize here. Rauschenbusch judged the deplorable misery of industrial-era cities to be the result of market forces that were inherently unjust. All wealth comes from injustice. "It is," he said, "not possible to get great wealth except by offending against justice" (*Righteousness of the Kingdom*, 212). For Rauschenbusch, the problem is thus wealth itself. He contends that the "prostitution of religion itself is brought about by the alliance of Christianity and wealth. Religion should do away with riches" (*Righteousness of the Kingdom*, 206). Wealth is the problem: socialism is the solution.

In my humble opinion, all this is gloriously wrong. But, it is even more important to address the deeper issue of the humanity of the poor themselves. In his own day, Rauschenbusch correctly pointed to the necessarily personal character of charity ("it is best administered by personal friends and neighbors") and lamented the rise of less personal philanthropic *organizations* to do the work of charity. "Modern charity divorces the gift and the giver. The giver does not know the receiver and the receiver does not know the giver." That Rauschenbusch is undoubtedly correct in this assessment is tragically ironic because his analysis and socialist solution leads to an even more impersonal agent—the state—an agent quite indifferent to the actual human condition of the poor. If one then speaks of a "preferential option for the poor" (more on this below), one no longer has in mind human hearts of compassion showing mercy to the needy and suffering, but rather the "poor" as a class that is naturally in conflict with the "rich." Instead of human beings reaching out in love to fellow human beings, we are now led to speak, as Article 25 of the United Nations Universal Declaration of Human Rights (1948) does, of universal "benefit rights":

> Everyone has the right to a standard of living adequate for the health and well-being of himself and of his family, including food, clothing, housing and medical care and necessary social services, and the right to security in the event of unemployment, sickness, disability, widowhood, old age or other lack of livelihood in circumstances beyond his control.

This long list of rights confuses *opportunity* with inherent *benefit rights*. It appears to seek guarantees for everyone, and the only way to conceive of this is to surrender all material goods into the hands of a benevolent redistributor. And, because only the state has the coercive, confiscatory power to accomplish that, it would require a surrender of individual liberty. Is this really preferable to voluntary charity? Is this price worth paying?

Even if we were willing to accept the bargain of Dostoyevsky's Grand Inquisitor (in *The Brothers Karamazov*) and trade in our freedom for material security, would this really benefit the poor? Can the devil really bake bread? Or, while asking for bread, would we get stones? Let's return for a moment to those late nineteenth-century dark and dismal days of industrial-age urban wretchedness. In his *The Tragedy of American Compassion*, a richly documented and provocative look at nineteenth-century charity and philanthropy, Marvin Olasky demonstrated that the problems of poor, urban underclasses were not, in the first place, economic. As an "rough-and-ready" example (given in 1992), if there are in the United States "7.5 million families below the poverty line and that on the average it would take a $12,000 income supplement to bring those families above the poverty line," poverty could be erased for a mere $90 billion (xii). But would it do any good? Would people change? Might it even tempt those whose income was just over the poverty line to do a little less and qualify for the $12,000 government gift? There are always unintended consequences; the sinful human mind is quite skillful at discovering incentives and disincentives that were unforeseen by social planners.

The story Olasky tells gives ample proof for thinking that the poor were treated much better in the nineteenth century because "human needs were answered by other human beings, not by bureaucracies" (xv), and those caring human beings were much better at holding the recipients of their charity responsible for their own improvement. In Olasky's words,

> The goal of charity workers, therefore, was not to press for governmental programs, but to show poor people how to move up while resisting enslavement to the charity of governmental or private masters. Charity leaders and preachers frequently spoke of freedom and showed how dependency was merely slavery with a smiling mask. . . . Freedom could be grasped only when individuals took responsibility. (112)

We do not have the space to chronicle this in greater detail; readers are encouraged to turn to Olasky's wonderful book for themselves. Suffice it here to list only a few of the numerous organizations that were set up to help the poor: the New York Association for Improving the Condition of the Poor, Societies for the Employment and Relief of the Poor, the Institution of Mercy, Ladies Christian Union, New York Foundling Hospital, Children's Aid Society, United Hebrew Charities, hundreds of inner-city missions, the Salvation Army, and the YMCA/YWCA. According to Olasky, there were some two thousand of these "points of light" in Baltimore, Chicago, and New York alone during 1890 (80). The point I wish to make here is that the "personal" response of charity, a response that was substantial and effective in the late nineteenth century, ought to precede government welfare programs. To say that charity is "personal" does not mean individual and private; much of the assistance given to the poor, along with the encouragement and guidance to become self-sufficient, came from the rich associational life of America citizens, including that of the churches and synagogues. By "personal" I have in mind the genuine care shown to the "person" of the poor; only the close intimate human connection provided by "charity" can treat the poor with the dignity and respect owed to them as responsible image bearers of God. Olasky summarizes this attitude nicely as he cautions his own readers not to apply his work into an excuse to "do nothing."

> These groups emphasized personal contact with the poor, even when some of their members were stunned by the first-hand experience. They refused to settle for the feed-and-forget principle or its equally depersonalizing but harsher opposite, the forget-and-don't-feed standard. They saw individuals made in the image of God, and when they saw someone acting disgracefully they responded, "You don't have to be that way. You're better than this. We expect more from you than an arm thrust out for food." Personal involvement became the hallmark of nineteenth-century compassion. (219–20)

Voluntary giving in love, we should add, along with gracious acceptance by a recipient, builds community. It is here that we experience the profoundest solidarity with fellow human beings. When both the giver and the receiver act *in love* they mutually enhance each other's humanity; a heartfelt "thank you" returns a blessing to the giver. The rich tradition of papal social teaching of the past one hundred years expressed this by the ideas of "friendship" (Leo XIII), "social charity" (Pius XI), and "a civilization of love" (Paul VI). John Paul II defined a "preferential option for the poor" as "a special form of primacy in the exercise of Christian charity." Contrary to Rauschenbusch, therefore, love comes before justice. "Love for others, and in the first place love for the poor, in whom the Church sees Christ himself," wrote John Paul, "is made concrete in the *promotion of justice*. Justice will never be fully attained unless people see in the poor person, who is asking for help in order to survive, not an annoyance or a burden, but an opportunity for showing kindness and a chance for greater enrichment" (*Centesimus Annus*, § 58; see Vatican Web site). Love is before justice and is its ground.

Finally, charity must be seen in a broader sociological perspective than merely as a matter of individual generosity. Because charity is voluntary and potentially more personal than government welfare, giving and receiving charity builds bonds of community that cannot be created by nor incorporated into the state. Such voluntary association leads to the creation of networks of protective structures and institutions (what is now usually called "civil society") that shield individuals from state encroachment on human liberty and the bonds of community. Contrary to the conventional view which holds that charity is the strategy of a selfish and individualistic culture "unwilling to pay its 'fair share' of taxes" to the federal government, it is in fact totalitarian regimes that cannot abide voluntary associations and active charity. According to that prescient nineteenth-century French observer of American mores, Alexis de Tocqueville, the American experiment is misrepresented when it is described as "individualistic"; it is in fact properly characterized as a form of "associationalism." In Tocqueville's words: "Despotism, which in its nature is fearful, sees the most certain guarantee of its own duration in the isolation of men, and it ordinarily puts all its care into isolating them. There is no vice of the human heart that agrees with it as much as selfishness: A despot readily pardons the governed for not loving him, provided that they do not love each other" (*Democracy in America*, trans. and ed. Harvey Mansfield and Delba Winthrop, 485; also see Barry Alan Shain, *The Myth of Individualism*).

The good word I have put in here for "charity" is inseparably linked with a commitment to the responsible use of human liberty as a check on the tendency for centralized state power to grow and grow. This too was seen by Tocqueville when he wrote the following: "Local freedoms, which make many citizens put value on the affection of their neighbors and those close to them, therefore constantly bring men closer to one another, despite the instincts that separate them, and force them to aid each other" (*Democracy in America*, 487).

What about a Safety Net? Should Reformed Christians Be Libertarians?

The characteristic response to giving charity a primacy over state-controlled welfare is that churches and voluntary associations are woefully inadequate to the massive task of poverty alleviation. Ron Sider, for example, states it bluntly: "[I]t would . . . be utterly wrong to suppose that civil society by itself can conquer poverty" (*Just Generosity*, 107). Sider may be correct about this, but when he estimates that it would cost each religious congregation an additional $382,000 per year for them to take over "the federal government's spending on just the four most basic programs for the poor," he overlooks two important factors. The first is efficiency; local religious-based charities could deliver services much more effectively. The second is that the entire load would not fall on religious congregations alone—Sider underestimates the creativity of Americans in forming new associations to meet community needs. Nonetheless, it is only honest to consider whether it is appropriate for government to provide a minimal safety net for those who fall between the cracks of civil society's resources.

Are there instances where only the weight and financial resources of government can address critical needs? The example that comes most frequently to people's minds is the natural disaster of a hurricane, earthquake, or tornado. Doesn't disaster relief require mobilization of people and other resources that only government can achieve? Perhaps, though it is not always clear that the US government's Federal Emergency Management Agency (FEMA) was more effective or efficient during New Orleans' Hurricane Katrina disaster in 2005 than the American Red Cross, America's Second Harvest (now Feeding America), or the numerous church-related relief agencies such as the Mennonite Central Committee, the Salvation Army, Southern Baptist Disaster Relief, Catholic Charities, Operation Blessing International, the Christian Reformed World Relief Committee (now World Renew), International Aid, and many others.

What about such federal government initiatives as Unemployment Insurance, Social Security, Medicare, and the like? Is it not a social, communal obligation for us to look out for the weakest, most vulnerable in our midst and seek their security and safety? Am I not my brother's keeper? Once we have separated our undoubted obligation of neighbor-love from state oversight of the care of our neighbor, these questions are matters for legitimate debate among Christians. Perhaps a minimal safety net for all people is best handled by government. *Perhaps* . . . or not. Our starting point should be neither a categorical yes nor an insistent no; Reformed Christians should neither be dogmatic libertarians nor incorrigible progressives. We need to ask questions about effectiveness and unintended consequences, which are matters of prudential wisdom rather than theological or moral principle. We also need to ask whether some important government initiatives run counter to the important principles of liberty and human dignity. Consider Alexis de Tocqueville's comments in his "Memoir on Pauperism": "I am deeply convinced that any permanent, regular, administrative system, whose aim will be to provide for the needs of the poor, will breed more miseries that it can cure" and "will deprave the population that it wants to help and comfort" (quoted in the preface to Cromartie, *Gaining Ground*). Abraham Kuyper agreed, insisting that "direct state aid . . . through distribution of money . . . be held to a minimum," concluding:

> Therefore I say that, unless you wish to undermine the position of the laboring class and destroy its natural resilience, the material assistance of the state should be confined to an absolute minimum. The continuing welfare of people and nation, including labor, lies only in powerful individual initiative. (*Problem of Poverty*, 72)

Resistance to state redistribution of resources is legitimate for Reformed Christians, even important, but we then do need to ask ourselves whether our resistance is a matter of principle or flows from less honorable motives such as indifference to the needs of the poor or even selfishness. In all of this, self-examination is much more necessary and helpful than accusation and judgment.

Let me conclude with a word or two about the church's task with respect to poverty. The church must zealously guard her independence from the state and political power. She needs to avoid getting drawn into being simply one more lobby group trying to

exert pressure in the world's power games. As an alternative structure, a structure with significant spiritual authority, the church
provides institutional counterweight to the state. Occasionally
having despotic rulers stand waiting in the snow for an audience
with the bishop is a salutary check on state power. Josef Stalin's
famous dismissive quip, "The Pope! How many divisions has he
got?" was answered in 1989 when Poland and other Eastern Bloc
countries broke the yoke of Soviet oppression. The Polish pope did
have many divisions or legions! Tyrants of course have no grasp of
the nature and power of these legionnaires of prayer. The church's
sword is that of Ephesians 6, "the sword of the Spirit," and not
that of the emperor or an imperial army. When the church is fulfilling its true mission—calling sinners to repentance and to new
life in Christ and then nurturing them in the faith—it *indirectly*
addresses the issue of poverty by helping to change human hearts
and habits. Poverty is in part a cultural and personal matter. As
Abraham Kuyper recognized years ago, it is possible to be poor in
earthly wealth and rich toward God. The converse is also tragically
true: many who are wealthy with respect to this world's goods are
poor toward God. When the Holy Spirit through the gospel re-
stores a person's sense of being an image bearer of God because he
shares the new and abundant life graciously given by God thanks
to Christ's atoning work, we are well on the road to bringing such
a person to a productive, satisfying life. The first thing the church
needs to do with respect to poverty is not to make apodictic pronouncements about specific governmental policies and strategies
to help the poor but to do its own proper task—be used of God to
save souls.

The church has one more task flowing out of its distinctive
mission—diaconal assistance. Diaconal aid has been a hallmark
of the Christian church's ministry from the time of the New Testament. Diaconal ministry is by the nature of the case ad hoc and
not systemic. That is its virtue—the goal is to help eliminate the

need by changing the hearts, circumstances, and life patterns of needy people. Genuine emergencies of course do happen, both personal and communal; people lose jobs and coastal states are hit with devastating hurricanes. At times like these the church—both the official church through its diaconal structures and the members though voluntary relief organizations—we cannot close its collective eyes, hearts, and wallets to those in need. Emergency, ad hoc relief is essential when disaster strikes.

In this chapter I have tried to portray a biblically framed approach to wealth and poverty that is much more complex than simple answers from the Left or the Right often present them. I emphasized respect for the individual responsibility of each image bearer of God alongside the obligations of human solidarity thanks to the social dimensions of the image. What emerges from this is a vision of human beings that celebrates the capacity we have to generate wealth through a stewardly use of creation's resources as well as the humanity-enhancing ability to give aid in love and receive it in grace. The psalmist asked God, "What is man that you are mindful of him?" (Ps. 8:4). Part of the answer is that we humans are "crowned . . . with glory and honor," the glory and honor of being "a little less than God" (v. 5 RSV). "The glory of God," wrote church father Irenaeus, "is man alive." That all men and women and children might have the glorious opportunity to be fully alive as God's image bearers—that is our Christian hope and prayer for the poor as well.

Discussion Questions

1. There are far too many poor people in the world. What is your Christian obligation to them? With finite resources at your disposal, how do you go about deciding which of the world's poor to accept responsibility for and what the extent of your obligation should be?

2. What are the most important lessons that Christian parents need to teach their children about poverty? Are you doing it and, if so, how?

3. What is your church doing about poverty? Assess the response.

Further Reading

Cromartie, Michael, ed. *Gaining Ground: New Approaches to Poverty and Dependency.* Washington, DC: Ethics and Public Policy Center, 1985.

Earthkeeping News: A Newsletter of the North American Coalition for Christianity and Ecology 7, no. 2 (January/February 1998): 1.

Kuyper, Abraham. *The Problem of Poverty.* Translated by James W. Skillen. Washington, DC: Center for Public Justice / Grand Rapids: Baker, 1991. Originally delivered as an address at the opening of the Social Congress on November 9, 1891 (Amsterdam, November 9–12, 1891) and then published that same year as *Het Sociale Vraagstuk en de Christelijke Religie* [The social question and the Christian religion].

Miller, Michael Matheson. "Street Smarts." *The American Spectator*, March 3, 2013. http://spectator.org/archives/2013/03/18/street-smarts.

National Religious Partnership for the Environment. "The Joint Appeal in Religion and Science: Statement by Religious Leaders at the Summit on Environment," New York City, New York, June 3, 1991. Available at http://fore.research.yale.edu/publications/statements/joint-appeal/.

Olasky, Marvin. *Renewing American Compassion: How Compassion for the Needy Can Turn Ordinary Citizens into Heroes.* New York: Free Press, 1996.

———. *The Tragedy of American Compassion.* Washington, DC: Regnery, 1992.

Shain, Barry Alan. *The Myth of American Individualism: The Protestant Origins of American Political Thought.* Princeton, NJ: Princeton University Press, 1994.

Sider, Ronald J. *Just Generosity: A New Vision for Overcoming Poverty in America.* 2nd ed. Grand Rapids: Baker, 2007. First published in 1999. Citations are to the 2007 edition.

Tocqueville, Alexis de. *Democracy in America.* Translated and edited by Harvey Mansfield and Delba Winthrop. Chicago: University of Chicago Press, 2000. Originally published in French in 2 vols., 1835–1840.

Epilogue
Economic Shalom

We live in amazing times where it is possible to talk to (while seeing!) loved ones on another continent, check the national and local weather, see how the Tigers–Blue Jays game at Comerica Park is progressing, and access the *Encyclopedia Britannica* or a nineteenth-century book on Google Books, all on a small handheld electronic device no bigger than a cigarette package. Who could have imagined that all this was possible from—sand! The human mind and the will to discover, to probe, to venture forth, to try out crazy ideas, and to risk—this is the greatest resource for good in the world. Two things, however, stand in the way of the human quest for improvement. The capacity of the human mind for discovery and stewardship requires liberty as its essential condition, and far too many of the world's multitudes live in destitute servitude and fear, not freedom. Sin and its consequences stand in the way of human flourishing. Furthermore, free people are also sinners and will abuse their freedom in countless ways that undermine human well-being, including their own.

In this volume I have put forth an unapologetic affirmation of a free-market economy set within a liberal democratic polity. This vision requires a moral people and also economic development and growth, a feature that troubles those who fret about the limits of earth's natural resources. "Are you not making an idol of markets, progress, and growth?" is the frequent response. So, let us be clear: our hope and confidence in the future is in God alone. It is precisely because I believe in God's providential rule over all things for the sake of his church that I can be open to the creativity and resourcefulness of free human beings. Because we trust in God alone, we can allow our fellow image bearers the liberty that God himself grants us.

If we want to see all of the seven billion plus people on planet Earth flourish, we need to ask, what is the alternative? The answer that is then given features the word *sustainability*. Very well, but does anyone really know what that involves? Isn't thinking that we are even capable of knowing this just one more example of the hubris that regularly gets us into trouble? I submit that it is impossible for anyone or any group to know the limits of our terrestrial resources and imprudent to attempt to restrict responsible exploration and use of them. In the 1970s Americans were told we would run out of oil and gas; in 2013 we are told that it is entirely possible for North America to be energy self-sufficient. New discoveries, new technologies, greater efficiencies, alternative sources of energy—the list goes on, and no one knows what the future will bring. We will only find out when we give permission to free and resourceful people to keep trying. For any group or a state to arbitrarily impose limits to this human activity would be to consign the poorest of the poor to their permanent fate. All Christians should find this unacceptable.

There is a deep irony in this attempt to curtail human creativity and resourcefulness. The same people who resolutely oppose economic growth tend to resist any curtailment in the growth of the state's power to intervene and to redistribute wealth. Christians who take the reality of sin seriously, so it seems to me, ought to do the exact opposite: encourage economic development and growth while advocating and working for a curtailment of state power and the accumulation of national debt. In other words, we should trust free people more and powerful people—or those lusting after power—less. To prevent any possible misunderstanding, I am not advocating a libertarian view that opposes government involvement in economic matters or regulation on principle; government regulation against fraud, harsh working conditions, environmental degradation, and so forth is appropriate and necessary. Nor am I am advocating indifference to the responsibilities of stewardly *use* of the world's resources. "Use" needs to be emphasized here; leaving resources dormant and unused is not stewardship; it is sloth. Lawful, responsible use must be tied to realistic expectations. We will not achieve perfect economic shalom in this age; we can, however, extend to countless others the relative and decidedly penultimate economic blessing that many of us enjoy. To envision that prospect requires a long-term rather than a short-term vision, and it begins with giving people the hope that comes from knowing they are God's image bearers who are redeemed in Christ.

This has concrete implications for the church's task in the world with respect to economic matters. The church has been given the task by our Lord to preach the gospel to the nations and make disciples. Its task, to state it differently, is to proclaim the good news that Christ came to give liberty to the captives, to set the prisoner free. When the church forsakes this task and becomes just one more power player in the world, one more lobby group petitioning for some state exercise of power unto a good end, it forsakes its task and its Lord. Tragically, the poor then have no one to preach good news to them and will continue to languish in their misery and suffering.

The astonishing wealth creation of the Western world (which has now spilled over into the East as well, notably in Japan, South Korea, Hong Kong, Singapore, India, and China) over the last two hundred plus years is also cause for wonder and awe. Masses have been lifted out of the drudgery, poverty, disease, and misery that are the default situation of postfall, sinful humanity and instead experience a *penultimate* and *imperfect* economic shalom. (To repeat, nearly one billion image-bearing human beings have been thus lifted out of extreme poverty in the decade from 1990 to 2000 alone.) As we look at our world we must never close our eyes to the far too many who are still destitute, but we do that in gratitude and hope: gratitude for what has been accomplished by sinful human beings and in hope that others may be set free to flourish. This is the test of our faith in God's providential, fatherly care. Grateful people, aware that all they have is a gift of God's grace, can and must be generous; they can't afford not to be.

Bibliography

Abela, Andrew V. "The Price of Freedom: Consumerism and Liberty in Secular Research and Catholic Teaching." *Journal of Markets and Morality* 10, no. 1 (Spring 2007): 7–25. http://www.marketsandmorality.com/index.php/mandm/article/view/260/251.

Accra Confession. Adopted by delegates of the World Alliance of Reformed Churches, 24th General Council, Accra, Ghana (2004). Available at http://www.wcrc.ch/node/469.

Baeur, P. T. "Ecclesiastical Economics: Envy Legitimized." Chap. 15 in *Is Capitalism Christian?* Edited by Franky Schaeffer. Westchester, IL: Crossway, 1985.

Bailey, Ronald. "Cracked Crystal Ball: Environmental Catastrophe Edition." *Reason*, December 30, 2010. http://reason.com/blog/2010/12/30/cracked-crystal-ball-environme.

Bavinck, Herman. *The Certainty of Faith*. Translated by Harry der Nederlanden. St. Catherines, ON: Paideia, 1980. Originally published in Dutch in 1901.

———. *The Christian Family*. Translated by Nelson D. Kloosterman. Grand Rapids: Christian's Library Press, 2012. Originally published in Dutch in 1908. Translation is based on the 2nd revised edition published in 1912.

———. "General Biblical Principles and the Relevance of Concrete Mosaic Law for the Social Question Today (1891)." Translated by John Bolt. *Journal of Markets and Morality* 13, no. 2 (Fall 2010): 411–46. http://www.marketsandmorality.com/index.php/mandm/article/view/103/97.

———. *Reformed Dogmatics*. 4 vols. Translated by John Vriend. Edited by John Bolt. Grand Rapids: Baker, 2003–2008. Originally published in Dutch in 1895–1901.

Bell, Daniel. *The Cultural Contradictions of Capitalism*. 20th anniversary ed. New York: Basic Books, 1996.

Bell, Rob. *Love Wins: A Book about Heaven, Hell, and the Fate of Every Person Who Ever Lived*. New York: HarperCollins, 2011.

Berger, Peter. *The Heretical Imperative: Contemporary Possibilities of Religious Affirmation*. Garden City, NY: Anchor Press, 1979.

Bethell, Tom. *The Noblest Triumph: Property and Prosperity through the Ages*. New York: St. Martin's Press, 1998.

Black, Robert A. "What Did Adam Smith Say about Self-Love?" *Journal of Markets and Morality* 9, no. 1 (Spring 2006): 7–34. http://www.marketsandmorality.com/index.php/mandm/article/view/310/299.

Blank, Rebecca M. "Viewing the Market through the Lens of Faith." In Rebecca M. Blank and William McGurn. *Is the Market Moral? A Dialogue on Religion, Economics, and Justice*, 11–56. Washington, DC: Brookings Institution Press, 2004.

Bolt, John. "*Catena sive Umbilicus*: A Christian View of Social Institutions." *Journal of Markets and Morality* 4, no. 2 (2001): 316–22. http://www.marketsandmorality.com/index.php/mandm/article/view/579/570.

———. *A Free Church, A Holy Nation: Abraham Kuyper's American Public Theology*. Grand Rapids: Eerdmans, 2001.

Calvez, Jean-Yves, and Jacques Perrin. *The Church and Social Justice: The Social Teaching of the Popes from Leo XIII to Pius XII (1878–1958)*. Translated by J. R. Kirwan. Chicago: Henry Regnery, 1961. This book includes all of the social encyclicals represented, except *Laborem Exercens* or *Centesimus Annus* or any encyclical published after 1961. Citations of encyclicals prior to 1961 and to *Centesimus Annus* in chapter 8, however, are to the versions on the Vatican Web site, http://www.vatican.va/.

Chilton, David. *Productive Christians in an Age of Guilt-Manipulators*. Tyler, TX: Institute for Christian Economics, 1981.

Claar, Victor V., and Robin J. Klay, *Economics in Christian Perspective: Theory, Policy and Life Choices*. Downers Grove, IL: InterVarsity Press, 2007.

Crespo, Ricardo F. "Controversy: Is Economics a Moral Science?" *Journal of Markets and Morality* 1, no. 2 (October 1998): 201–11. http://www.marketsandmorality.com/index.php/mandm/article/view/3/2.

Cromartie, Michael, ed. *Gaining Ground: New Approaches to Poverty and Dependency.* Washington, DC: Ethics and Public Policy Center, 1985.

De Soto, Hernando. *The Mystery of Capital: Why Capitalism Triumphs in the West and Fails Everywhere Else.* New York: Basic Books, 2000.

Earthkeeping News: A Newsletter of the North American Coalition for Christianity and Ecology 7, no. 2 (January/February 1998): 1.

Echeverria, Eduardo J. "Bavinck on the Family and Integral Human Development." *Journal of Markets and Morality* 16, no. 1 (Spring 2013): 219–37.

Eglinton, James. *Trinity and Organism: Towards a New Reading of Herman Bavinck's Organic Motif.* Edinburgh: T&T Clark, 2012.

Ehrlich, Paul R. *The Population Bomb.* New York: Ballantine Books, 1968.

Eliot, T. S. *The Idea of a Christian Society.* London: Faber and Faber, 1939.

Enns, Peter. *The Evolution of Adam: What the Bible Does and Does Not Say about Human Origins.* Grand Rapids: Brazos, 2012.

Freedman, David R. "Woman, a Power Equal to a Man." *Biblical Archeology Review* 9 (1983): 56–58.

Friedman, Milton, and Rose Friedman. *Free to Choose: A Personal Statement.* New York: Harcourt Brace Jovanovich, 1980.

Gay, Craig M. *With Liberty and Justice for Whom? The Recent Evangelical Debate over Capitalism.* Grand Rapids: Eerdmans, 1991.

Hart, David Bentley. *Atheist Delusions: The Christian Revolution and Its Fashionable Enemies.* New Haven and London: Yale University Press, 2009.

Hayek, Friedrich A. "Kinds of Order in Society." *New Individualist Review* 3, no. 2 (1964). Reprinted in *The Politicization of Society.* Edited by Kenneth S. Templeton Jr., 501–23. Indianapolis: Liberty Press, 1979. Also available online at http://oll.libertyfund.org/index.php?option=com_staticxt&staticfile=show.php%3Ftitle=2136&layout=html#chapter_195376.

King, Alexander, and Bertrand Schneider. *The First Global Revolution: A Report by the Council of the Club of Rome.* New York: Pantheon Books, 1991. http://ia700408.us.archive.org/31/items/TheFirstGlobalRevolution/ TheFirstGlobalRevolution.pdf.

Kristol, Irving. *Two Cheers for Capitalism.* New York: Basic Books, 1978.

Klos, Jan. "Spontaneous Order versus Organized Order." *Journal of Markets and Morality* 6, no. 1 (Spring 2003): 161–76. http://www.marketsandmorality.com/index.php/mandm/article/view/494/485.

Küng, Hans. "Justification Today: An Introductory Chapter to the New Edition" (1980), translated by Edward Quinn. In *Justification: The Doctrine of Karl Barth and a Catholic Reflection.* Translated by Thomas Collins, Edmund E. Tolk, and David Granskou. Philadelphia: Westminster Press, 1981. First published in English in 1964.

Kuyper, Abraham. *Lectures on Calvinism.* Grand Rapids: Eerdmans, 1931. Originally published as *Calvinism: Six Stone-Lectures.* Amsterdam-Pretoria, Höveker & Wormser; New York: Fleming H. Revell, 1899. Available online at http://www.reformationalpublishingproject.com/ pdf_books/Scanned_Books_PDF/LecturesOnCalvinism.pdf.

———. *The Problem of Poverty.* Translated by James W. Skillen. Washington, DC: Center for Public Justice / Grand Rapids: Baker, 1991. Originally delivered as an address at the opening of the Social Congress on November 9, 1891 (Amsterdam, November 9–12, 1891) and then published that same year as *Het Sociale Vraagstuk en de Christelijke Religie* [The social question and the Christian religion].

———. "Sphere Sovereignty." Inaugural address at the founding of the Free University of Amsterdam, October 20, 1880. In *Abraham Kuyper: A Centennial Reader.* Edited by James D. Bratt, 461–90. Grand Rapids: Eerdmans, 1998.

Larson, David. "Adam Smith: Selfishness or Self-Interest." *Spectrum*, January 23, 2009. http://spectrummagazine.org/node/1368.

Levinson, Marc. *The Great A&P and the Struggle for Small Business in America.* New York: Hill and Wang, 2013.

Meadows, Donella H., Dennis L. Meadows, Jørgen Randers, and William W. Behrens III. *Limits to Growth: A Report for the Club of Rome's Project on the Predicament of Mankind.* New York: Universe Books, 1972. An abbreviated version is available online at http://www.bibliotecapleyades.net/sociopolitica/esp_sociopol_clubrome6.htm. Updates were published in 1992 and 2002, and a forecast for the next forty years was published in 2012.

McIntyre, Douglas A., Samuel Weigley, Alexander E. M. Hess, and Michael B. Sauter. "Eight Retailers That Will Close the Most Stores." 24/7 Wall St., January 29, 2013. http://247wallst.com/special-report/2013/01/29/eight-retailers-that-will-close-the-most-stores/.

Meilander, Gilbert, ed. *Working: Its Meaning and Limits.* Notre Dame, IN: University of Notre Dame Press, 2000. A most helpful anthology of readings on the meanings of work, the limits of work, and rest.

Miller, Michael Matheson. "Street Smarts." *The American Spectator*, March 3, 2013. http://spectator.org/archives/2013/03/18/street-smarts.

Minogue, Kenneth R. *Alien Powers: The Pure Theory of Ideology.* 2nd ed. New Brunswick, NJ: Transaction, 2007. First published in 1985.

National Religious Partnership for the Environment. "The Joint Appeal in Religion and Science: Statement by Religious Leaders at the Summit on Environment," New York City, New York, June 3, 1991. Available at http://fore.research.yale.edu/publications/statements/joint-appeal/.

Neuhaus, Richard John. *Doing Well and Doing Good: The Challenge to the Christian Capitalist.* New York: Doubleday, 1992. This book is an extended meditation on John Paul II's 1991 encyclical *Centesimus Annus* (cited as *CA* in chap. 6), which is included in this work, in condensed form, as an appendix, pages 285–304. Citations of this encyclical in chapter 6 are to the condensed Doubleday version; citations in chapter 8 are to the version on the Vatican Web site, http://www.vatican.va/.

———. "Why Wait for the Kingdom? The Theonomist Temptation." *First Things* (May 1990): 13–21. http://www.firstthings.com/article/2007/08/002-why-wait-for-the-kingdom-the-theonomist-temptation-38.

Niebuhr, H. Richard. *The Kingdom of God in America.* Middletown, CT: Wesleyan University Press, 1988. First published in 1937.

Norberg, Johan. *In Defense of Global Capitalism.* Washington, DC: Cato Institute, 2003.

Novak, Michael. *The Spirit of Democratic Capitalism.* New York: American Enterprise Institute / Simon & Schuster, 1982.

Olasky, Marvin. *Renewing American Compassion: How Compassion for the Need Can Turn Ordinary Citizens into Heroes.* New York: Free Press, 1996.

———. *The Tragedy of American Compassion.* Washington, DC: Regnery, 1992.

Pellissier-Tanon, Arnoud, and José Moreira. "Can Social Justice Be Achieved?" *Journal of Markets and Morality* 10, no. 1 (Spring 2007): 143–55. http://www.marketsandmorality.com/index.php/mandm/article/view/266/257.

Rauschenbusch, Walter. *Christianizing the Social Order.* New York: MacMillan, 1912.

———. *Christianity and the Social Crisis.* New York: Macmillan, 1907.

———. *The Righteousness of the Kingdom.* Edited by Max Stackhouse. Nashville: Abingdon, 1968.

Ridderbos, Herman. *The Coming of the Kingdom.* Translated by H. de Jongste. Edited by Raymond O. Zorn. Philadelphia: P&R, 1962.

Ryan, John Julian. "Humanistic Work: Its Philosophical and Cultural Implications." In *A Matter of Dignity: Inquiries into the Humanization of Work.* Edited by W. J. Heisler and John W. Houck. Notre Dame, IN: University of Notre Dame Press, 1977.

Sayers, Dorothy. "Why Work?" In *Letters to a Diminished Church: Passionate Arguments for the Relevance of Christian Doctrine*, 125–46. Nashville: W Pubishing Group, 2004. A compact and practical homily on the dignity of work, originally delivered on April 23, 1942, at a time of great scarcity and conflict during World War II.

Schlossberg, Herbert. *Idols for Destruction.* Nashville: Thomas Nelson, 1983.

Schneider, John R. *The Good of Affluence: Seeking God in a Culture of Wealth.* Grand Rapids: Eerdmans, 2002.

Shain, Barry Alan. *The Myth of American Individualism: The Protestant Origins of American Political Thought.* Princeton, NJ: Princeton University Press, 1994.

Shepherd, Norman. "Postmillennialism." In *Zondervan Pictorial Encyclopedia of the Bible.* Vol. 5. Edited by Merrill C. Tenney, 822–23. Grand Rapids: Zondervan, 1975.

Schulz, David P. "Top 100 Retailers." *STORES* magazine, July 2013. http://www.stores.org/STORES%20Magazine%20July%202013/ top-100-retailers.

Sider, Ronald J. *Rich Christians in an Age of Hunger: A Biblical Study.* Nashville: Thomas Nelson, 2005. Originally published in 1977. Citations are to the 2005 edition.

———. *Just Generosity: A New Vision for Overcoming Poverty in America.* 2nd ed. Grand Rapids: Baker, 2007. First published in 1999. Citations are to the 2007 edition.

Simon, Julian. *Hoodwinking the Nation.* New Brunswick, NJ: Transaction, 1999.

Sirico, Robert. *Defending the Free Market: The Moral Case for a Free Economy.* Washington, DC: Regnery, 2012.

Sharifi, Jim. "How Patriotic Is Your Car?" *U.S. News and World Report,* June 30, 2011. http://usnews.rankingsandreviews.com/cars-trucks/ how_american_is_your_car/.

Smith, Adam. *An Inquiry into the Nature and Causes of the Wealth of Nations.* Edited by Edwin Cannan. Modern Library of the World's Best Books. New York: Modern Library, 1965. Originally published in 1776.

———. *The Theory of Moral Sentiments.* Edited by Knud Haakonssen. Cambridge Texts in the History of Philosophy. Cambridge: Cambridge University Press, 2002. Originally published in 1759.

Sojourners magazine. http://www.sojo.net/. First published in 1971 under the original title of *The Post-American.* Founding editor-in-chief, Jim Wallis.

Sowell, Thomas. *Basic Economics: A Common Sense Guide to the Economy.* 4th ed. New York: Basic Books, 2011. First published in 2000.

———. *A Conflict of Visions: Ideological Origins of Political Struggles.* New York: William Morrow, 1987.

———. *The Quest for Cosmic Justice.* New York: Free Press, 1999.

Tocqueville, Alexis de. *Democracy in America.* Translated and edited by Harvey Mansfield and Delba Winthrop. Chicago: University of Chicago Press, 2000. Originally published in French in 2 vols., 1835–1840.

"Towards the End of Poverty." *The Economist,* June 1, 2013. http://www. economist.com/news/leaders/21578665-nearly-1-billion-people-have-been-taken-out-extreme-poverty-20-years-world-should-aim.

The United Nations Universal Declaration of Human Rights (1948). http:// www.un.org/en/documents/udhr/.

Van Drunen, David. "The Importance of the Penultimate: Reformed Social Thought and the Contemporary Critiques of the Liberal Society." *Journal of Markets and Morality* 9, no. 2 (2006): 219–49. http://www. marketsandmorality.com/index.php/mandm/article/view/281/272.

———. *Living in God's Two Kingdoms: A Biblical Vision for Christianity and Culture.* Wheaton: Crossway, 2010.

Warfield, Benjamin B. *Perfectionism, Part 1* and *Perfectionism, Part 2.* In *The Works of Benjamin B. Warfield.* Vols. 7–8. New York: Oxford University Press, 1932. Reprinted: Grand Rapids: Baker, 1991.

Weiser, Jay, "The Big Store: The Mythology of Small Business Meets a Retailing Giant." Review of *The Great A&P and the Struggle for Small Business in America* by Marc Levinson, *The Weekly Standard,* April 29, 2013, 33–35. http://www.weeklystandard.com/articles/big-store_718089.html.

Wikipedia contributors. "Simon-Ehrlich wager." *Wikipedia, The Free Encyclopedia.* http://en.wikipedia.org/wiki/Simon-Ehrlich_wager. Accessed May 15, 2013.

Wolterstorff, Nicholas. *Until Justice and Peace Embrace: The Kuyper Lectures for 1981 Delivered at the Free University of Amsterdam.* Grand Rapids: Eerdmans, 1983.

About the Author

John **Bolt** (PhD, University of St. Michael's College) is professor of systematic theology at Calvin Theological Seminary in Grand Rapids, Michigan, where he has taught for more than twenty years. For Dr. Bolt, the task of the systematic theologian is to pay attention to the big picture of the Christian faith, to summarize the grand truths of Scripture in a coherent way, and listen closely to the voices of important theologians throughout church history. His goal is to communicate the vision of the Christian faith from a Reformed perspective. Previously, Dr. Bolt taught at Calvin College (Grand Rapids, Michigan) and Redeemer University College (Ancaster, Ontario). He has served as pastor of Christian Reformed churches in Pencticton and Kelowna, British Columbia. Dr. Bolt is the author of *The Christian Story and the Christian School*, *Stewards of the Word*, and *A Free Church, a Holy Nation: Abraham Kuyper's Public Theology* and is the editor of numerous books, including Herman Bavinck's four-volume English edition of *Reformed Dogmatics*. He is married to Ruth and has three children and nine grandchildren.

Made in the USA
Lexington, KY
03 November 2014